MW00928256

Endorsements:

Katie Dunstan is skilled as she weaves the Ancient paths and the New and Living Way marked with fresh revelation and prophetic encounter. Her penned words resonate with the heart cry and the "burning in our bones" for many of us who have longed to see First Nations Arise in God ordained purpose. Katie articulates the rumble that is being felt and heard in the spirit in every indigenous land as awakened Sons shift into destiny. The keys that Katie addresses are unlocking the ancient paths long given by the Creator to show us the way forward in this new era. Truly a book for this hour!

To Katie, sister of my heart.
Miigech!

Mary M. Faus
Anishinaabekwe Thunder Sky Woman Turtle Island
Indigenous global Watch USA

I am so excited about Katie Dunstan's book 'Ancient Keys to a New Sound - Rising from the Land'. The prophetic voices of our land are releasing keys, strategies and vision from the Lord that are for such a time as this, and as we listen with open hearts of humility, the sound of the Lord roaring with passion for this nation of Australia. Our nation is in great need of revival and I believe this ground-breaking work is giving voice to strategic keys needed in this hour. We need a new wineskin for new wine. Lift up your heads, for the King of glory is coming!

Katherine Ruonala
Senior Leader Glory City Church Network
Founder and Facilitator of the Australian Prophetic Council

"When Katie asked me if I would endorse her book, before even looking at the manuscript the Lord spoke to me "Lana, this book will be one of the keys to unlock My plans and purposes in the Great Southland of the Holy Spirit" and that is EXACTLY what this book is. It is a precious and weighty key God is going to use to bring forth a great unlocking. Reading the revelation God has given Katie around the new sound rising from the land, the positioning and empowering of the First Nation people to take their place like never before, the healing, the recompense, the revelation contained in these pages, have been penned with such articulation of His heart, nature and the weight of His presence. This book will ignite the fire within you for what God is doing in this era in exponential ways. What an incredible gift you have given to us Katie, thank you! There is incredible fire on these pages. This is a book to continue to "go back to" for this new era in all the Lord has planned for our beautiful nation."

Lana Vawser
Author, Prophetic Voice, Speaker lanavawser.com

At a time when there is need for much hope, here emerges a robust, powerful and exuberant sound from Katherine Dunstan. She is a radiant prophet and lover of God who invites us heavenward into an awakening of love for Jesus Christ. Her authentic encounters with Him and with His angels, draw us into realms of glory where the Bride emerges on earth with the kind of courage that was intended for her.
One can almost hear the decrees in each chapter, rising together as one voice, with the sole purpose of shifting atmospheres and seeing transformation in lives.
This book is rich with biblical truth and will awaken the readers to the sound of the First Nations beloved people for such a time as this! For every believer looking to be supercharged with love for Jesus and to be renewed in hope as part of His end time move in Australia - I highly recommend this book to you.
Fini de Gersigny Co-Founder Jubilee Church Sydney

Katherine Dunstan has marked out for every reader a most powerful journey that walks us through the raw beauty of her authentic encounters with the Lord. The book Ancient Keys (to a New Sound Rising in the Land) is charged with faith in God and drips with the new wine of encountering Jesus from Gethsemane to His risen and glorious throne. It will draw the reader not only into a deeper and sweeter union with Jesus by the Spirit, but also into engaging from the dominion of union with God in releasing His Love and fire over an ancient land that is so ready to yield to the new sound of the voices of the land. A seer and Tidda like Katherine with such pure vulnerability, has invited us in a most compelling way to participate in the response to prayer and decree of life over the nation of Australia and her magnificently diverse people. The ancient keys are here - now open up you ancient doors and let the King of Glory have His way through you!

Isi de Gersigny
Co-Founder Jubilee Church Sydney
Founding member Australian Prophetic Council

This book will excite, inspire, encourage and equip you to embrace God's love and glorious destiny for Australia, her First Nation's people and First Nation's people across the globe. Please take time to read and re-read this book and explore the depths of insight and revelation contained in it. Share it with the First Nations loved ones you know.

This book has the potential to be a catalyst to begin a movement of First Nations people across the globe. Katie has a profound and vital message of how God has uniquely called and gifted First Nation's people and given them authority in the land. She shares an understanding of the powerful impact the songs and sounds belonging to the First Nation's people have in any land.

With wisdom and prophetic insight she also gives revelation of how crucial these sounds are in bringing revival and restoration to a nation. Through her powerful encounters with the Lord, Katie releases through this book the fire of the Lord's love and passion that will ignite your heart to rise up and be part of revival and reformation for your nation.

This book is a prophetic call for all Australians in this 'New Era of His Glory' to rise together in unity and love. This is a timely message from heaven to be heard and embraced. Don't miss this glorious invitation and explanation of how to participate in God's destiny call to the people and land of Australia and indeed, for First Nation's people and lands across the globe.

Cheryl Lindley ARC Global; Shift the Nations

"Ancient Keys to a New Sound Rising from the Land" is an amazing gift to the body of Christ. All Christians – both Indigenous and non-Indigenous, all need to understand God's heart and destiny for the First Nations people and the land. Every believer needs to understand how to step into revival, reformation and be an agent of transformation and fire for the healing in their land. We need to know how to activate and use ancient keys in this new era. I have enjoyed reading Katie Dunstan's book. It really does carry her heart as well as an amazing Indigenous prophetic mantle to shift this nation into to its divine purpose given by God, before the foundation of the world.

Katie has given you an excellent resource to equip you with biblical insight and strategic patterns to enable you to go forward and emerge in the fullness of your destiny too. You will be blessed by her prophetic insights of being 'grafted in', healing of the land and impacted to be a part of your next generational transfer.

Her strategic decrees, prayers and scriptures will help you activate God strategies for you and your land. Lord is indeed 're-shaping the face of the land. Re-setting the foundation of old to reveal the found nation of now.' Truly it is the time for you and I 'to come forth'! It is such an honour for you and I to be a part of this move of God.

What a revelation and mandate for every Christian (regardless what nation you live in) as well as the First Nations mothers and fathers in the body of Christ.

Bruce Lindley Founding Apostle ARC Global Apostolic Community

Whenever God shapes us to release a timely message, He does a thorough job of preparing the soil of our hearts, so the fruit of that word can be incredible! In Katie Dunstan, we see a woman who has been diligent in working with the Lord of the Harvest to prepare the soil for a bumper crop. Katie is a true prophet of Australia and of the Indigenous people of our nation. She signals with clarity, the call to build and rebuild, the foundations for a nation-wide move of God. Katie is a gifted seer who understands the times and seasons. She recognises that the healing of the land and our original elders and people, are a pivotal part of the army of God in this hour. I love her heart and this book is a great big piece of her heart! Her voice and message are undeniably needed. I have every reason to believe that this highly prophetic message will turn the hearts of our fathers to the sons and vice versa. Thank you, Katie for your work and this extraordinary book.

Maria Mason, Senior Leader, Tribe Byron Bay, and the Heart Revolution Network.

I recommend this book to every leader, leaders in training and all our First Nations brothers and sisters. This book is strategic in positioning and repositioning the body of Christ.

Firstly to our indigenous brothers and sisters in the Lord, this book will help you to position yourselves in place to be used by God, an army called to arise and lead for God's Glory in this New Era. This book is especially a powerful tool to help the non-Indigenous Australian church understand the importance of joining in and running together with our Indigenous brothers and sisters in unity, forming one new man. This is a unity that will see an awakening in our nation and revival coming to all the four corners of Australia. Together we win. Australia for Jesus.

Apostle Jimmy Njiino Senior Leader Victory Life Church Toowoomba NSW Australia

Psalm 97:1, 5, and 6 "The Lord reigns. Let the earth rejoice. Let her Islands and her coastlands be very glad...... The mountains melt like wax before the presence of our God. HEAVEN declares HIS righteousness and all people will see HIS glory and HIS brilliance." Australia and her First Nations people have long had the eye of Jehovah Sabaoth (The Lord of Hosts), and the mountains which seem consuming, around them will melt like wax before the Lord of many Hosts.

Keys unlock doors, doors transition us to another place and this book is a revelation of both. Moses had "influence" with God, and my prayer over this book is that every Aboriginal woman in this Country will have her head lifted to know....she can influence Yahweh Adoni (The Lord).

As a Gomeroi Pastor I am hand in hand with you Katie. Just like King David, I share your confidence...that we will see this goodness of God in our days of living. This book is more than just words that incorporate the magnificence of our culture, purpose and our God.

The words, the movements, the song, the dressing and the positioning: - this is a call to the Warriors across the lands.

Pastor Katie, you move in the gift and office of a Prophet, but I say that this book is a weapon of intercession! There is such profound, yet humble words and decrees that are piercing through the bone and marrow - the flesh and the Spirit.
This writing is releasing prophetic intercession into the realms for spiritual breakthrough across our nation.

Tina Maybury Gomeroi Pastor; Part of Global Intercessors

"One of the great distinctions of the God of the bible from many other so-called Gods is that Elohim is both the God of the heavens and the earth. To disconnect God and His mission from both realms is to misrepresent Him accurately.
For many years, it has been my conviction that the body of Christ in Australia would never be able to rise into the fullness of her destiny unless and until the First Nations people were able to stand equally amongst the rest of their brothers and sisters. There is an undeniable redemptive grace that rests powerfully upon the First Nations people of this great southland.

Many prayers and effort have been invested, particularly over the last several decades, to raise our First Nations brothers and sisters to take their place in the body of Christ. By the grace of God, we are now seeing a powerful move of the Holy Spirit amid the First Nations people in not just revival and signs and wonders, but also in the raising of fivefold leaders. Apostles, prophets, pastors, teachers and evangelists from within the First Nations people are rising with a powerful anointing to proclaim, demonstrate and expand the Kingdom.

We are in a season of great prophetic fulfilment and it is marvellous to see. Katherine Dunstan is a First Nations woman who is a powerful kingdom prophet, who represents the King and His kingdom so well. As you read and journey through this book that reads as a testimony of the breaking in of God amongst and through Katherine's life, you will be inspired and empowered to capture a dimension of the heart of God for this time, and also discover how connected the work of the kingdom is to land and people."

David Balestri
A member of the national leadership team of the
Australian Prophetic Council.

It was a privilege to read "Ancient Keys to A New Sound - Rising from The Land". This book has helped me feel connected in a deeper way to Australia as it carries unique insights that only an owner of the land can have. It has increased my understanding in a gentle and profound way. Pastor Katie's revelations and prayer points in this book are both practical and anointed and carry such a laser focussed authority. She writes with wisdom, discernment, grace and love. It truly felt like I was invited into receiving ancient keys to our great South Land of the Holy Spirit! I highly recommend reading the golden nuggets contained in this book.

Roma Waterman
Heartsong Prophetic Alliance; Heartsong Creative
Academy

I have thoroughly enjoyed Katie sharing her heart and passion for her people, I am sure like me, naturally and spiritually your eyes will be opened wide as she articulates prophetically with words and pictures of the Spirit lead life. This leaves us with a clear collective picture of First Nation people along with us, all living and functioning in His Kingdom here on the earth. As we travel through this book with her, God's extravagant love and power invades us, allowing us the possibility to enjoy the same sense of fruitfulness and prophetic insight. What else can I say but well done good and faithful servant! I have so enjoyed this outstanding epistle of Love, Grace and Power.

Judy McIntyre Global Mission

Right from the very beginning of this book Katie began taking me on this wonderful creative journey, that doesn't just give me insight into the history and position of her First Nation family, but with her ease of comfort in knowing who she is in the Person of Christ, she paints this amazing picture with words and Spirit, drawing every tribe and tongue of God's family of Believers, to want to invade every corner of our nation and nations with delegated Grace, Power, and Love, through the same spirit that that Katie herself appears to carry. Even if you don't believe it now, by the time you read this book you will believe that the Kingdom of God is righteousness joy and peace in the Holy Spirit. The impartation of these pages into your heart and soul, is going to leave you with a sense of righteousness, joy and peace, and the sense that I too can be what God wants me to be, to release a move of His Spirit.

Fergus McIntyre   Global Mission

My Tidda Katie Dunstan has written an informative and inspiring book about worship and the vital role of the voice of First Nations people groups in Australia, the Great Southland of the Holy Spirit, and across the globe to see nations rise to revival, reformation and transformation in this era. Her refreshing and insightful interpretation of the scripture is testament to Katie's own personal journey. Katie is a living example of what she has written. She has experienced firsthand the amazing transformation of the Spirit that comes when we surrender to Jesus Christ our Saviour. I encourage the reader to *allow Katie's prophetic words to revolutionise your thinking and awaken your senses, and help you to navigate God's plan to usher in revival, reformation and transformation.*

You will be blessed by Katie's insightful prophetic word about the 'Ancient Blueprint.' Katie encourages God's people to understand the times and seasons, and to be more aware of our responsibility as Kingdom people to worship unashamedly and fervently as Jesus mentioned in John 4, that the true worshippers will worship in Spirit and in truth. Jesus declared that he is enthroned on the praises of his people, and his Kingdom is within us. Katie encourages us to operate in the 5 fold ministry because "All" things are possible when we believe, and the 5 fold ministries is for the perfecting of the saints. I am a First Nation Indigenous woman from the Malanbarra Yidingji people of the Goldsborough Valley, in North Queensland and I understand the urgency of Katie's prophetic word to the First Nation people. There is a mandate upon us to hear the voice of the 'Ancient of Days' (Yahweh God of Holiness) saying, 'arise and claim your inheritance.' My Tidda Katie hears and prophesies that, a new sound of affirmation, worship and praise will arise from the hearts of those who believe! I highly recommend Katie's book, Ancient Keys to a New Sound Rising from the Land. God bless! Love

Robyn Green-Beezley
Indigenous Christian Leader; Singer Song Writer;
Preacher for over 40 years

Wow!! I was so excited and encouraged to read "Ancient Keys to a New Sound Rising from the Land". I first want to congratulate Katie and thank her for her courage to pen what the Lord has been saying. As a fellow Indigenous Christian leader in our nation I remember hearing long ago visiting international ministries and prominent Australian ministries, all release prophetic words about the destiny of our First Nations peoples in Australia. I believe what Katie has skilfully illustrated within these pages will be a blessing and contribution to help "put the flesh on the bones" of the army that is arising in Lord for such a time as this. The many prophetic words and revelations that Katie has shared here are the Lord's invitation to the bride, to move in a season of new understanding, and new relationships to take new territories for the Kingdom of God and our soon coming King, Christ Jesus.

Nathan Seden
Next Generation Australian Indigenous Christian Leader

When I started reading this book my spirit and mouth screamed at the same time "Yes, finally!" like there was some powerful divine unlocking taking place in its release. I could feel the Fathers heart on this, that it's been long overdue that First Nations prophets arose to be the ones at the head of the pack waving in this great and fierce promised move of God in our nation. You see the enemy has wanted them silent and shut up and not part of their own lands redemption story but those days are over and there is a clarion call going out right now for the mothers, fathers, auntys, uncles, sons, and daughters of this great southern land to stand to their feet and prophesy in the wave. Right now in the hour of our nations greatest conflict there is also the converging of many many words and utterances over this great southland crashing upon our shores and reminding us once again of who we are. Yes, this book is more timely for this hour than any of us could have known but as you read it's pages you will feel what I did - apathy break off, a fresh stirring to pray and intercede for this land and her people, and a cry that will shake you to your bones of "Yes finally!" Because the harvest has hit our shores.

Nate Johnston
Author of The Wild Ones

KATIE DUNSTAN

ANCIENT KEYS
to a
NEW SOUND
RISING FROM THE LAND

PROPHETIC INSIGHTS TO UNLOCK
THE NEW ERA

Cover design by Joshua Halls ROAR KINGDOM CREATIVE

ISBN 9798776200885
Published by Breakfree Australia

Dedication:

*F*or you Jesus! It's all for you. I am honoured to journey life's ancient pathways with you, while on track to eternity. To make tracks and leave spiritual footprints on the land with you Jesus, is my delight. Created in your image from the dust of the land, our interconnectedness is divine.

It is my honour to pass on the revelation knowledge that you give to me, and to share stories of our encounters and adventures. I share my journey with the hope that it leads people into new dimensions of your love Lord Jesus, through genuine relationship with you, loving you and deeply knowing you Jesus.

Here's to discovering ancient love, and creating new song-lines of wild worship, infused with forever love. Jesus, it's all for you. Katie x

Acknowledgements:

$\mathcal{A}$ huge thank you to my kind husband, a scholarly Apostolic Bible teacher for keeping me theologically sound, helping me to communicate my heart with greater clarity, and championing me from the inception to the birthing of this book. I honour you my Love.

Thank you to our First Nations Generals in the Faith, Apostolic Father and Mother in this nation: Pastors Tim and Di Edwards. Thank you for loving, supporting, building into me and walking with me through my prophetic journey. Thank you for raising up the next generation of First Nation leaders, and for being on the frontline battlefield as you warfare and lead our nation into many victories. Only God knows the intensity and cost of those battles and those victories. I weep at the weight of this and well up with triumphant joy, all at the same time. The best is yet to come!

Jenny Haggar, General in the Faith and Mother of Nations, I salute you! Thank you from my heart, for walking with and championing me and all our First Nations people, here in Australia, across the Great Southland of the Holy Spirit, and in many nations. Thank you for having the courage, strength, humility and obedience to go into our pain, again and again, for valuing and empowering us to rise and lead; for pushing back the powers of darkness to break through into victories for us all. What a gift you are to me personally, and to the Body of Christ.

Thank you Bruce and Cheryl Lindley for unlocking and releasing me into new realms of the prophetic; I just love to move in those realms with you. Thank you for loving and championing me, for continually challenging me to be true to the new wine skin, and for modelling Apostolic and Prophetic Fathering and Mothering so very well.

You are true Mothers and Fathers raising up generations of sons and daughters, and Apostles and Prophets around the globe. I honour and love you both dearly.

Katherine Ruonala, thank you for welcoming me into relationship with the Australian Prophetic Council family and being just a phone call away.

Sue Connell, thank you and Ray for interceding, warring and taking spiritual ground for both my husband and I. Thank you for editing this book.

Thank you to:
Fini and Isi de Gersigny: for leading and loving so well. I am continually learning and gleaning from you both.

Maria Mason: for your wisdom, sound guidance and for being so real.

David Balestri: for continually showing me the Father's heart, in the way that you lead and inspire me to keep becoming.

Lana Vawser: for being so kind to me, encouraging me and modelling genuine humility so well.

Diane Pearce, thank you for believing in the gift on my life and for mentoring me in the prophetic, healing and deliverance.

Roma Waterman: for your kind and generous assistance with the book cover, and your heart for our people. Thank you Joshua Halls for capturing the elements and vision to create the cover design.

Thank you Nate Johnston for the authentic fire that you carry for our First Nations people.

A special thank you to my heart sister Mary Faus. From a Gomeroi Murri Yinnar (Aboriginal woman of Gomeroi tribe) to my kindred Anishinaabekwe, Thunder Sky Woman, Turtle Island. I say Maarubaa nginda! (Thank you!)

A very special thank you to some treasured people in my life who love so well and who I highly value and appreciate: My deadly Tiddas Tina Maybury and Robyn Green-Beezley. Tina you have been a safe place and wise counsel; my brothers Nathan Seden and Jimmy Njiino for the solid Indigenous Apostolic leaders you are; Ferg (Big Dadda) and Mumma Jude McIntyre for loving me and imparting so much into my life, and for way too much to write here; Robyn and Alan Ross for your invaluable love and wisdom; and Cate Lewis for championing me. You may never know the impact your love and sheer kindness has had on me.

CONTENTS

PART 1:   FIRST NATIONS UNLOCKED

PART 2:   UNITY FAMILY ONENESS

Foreword by Tim Edwards

$\mathcal{A}$s an Australian Indigenous Christian Leader now Elder for many years, we have heard so many prophetic words in relation to Aboriginal and Torres Strait Islanders taking our rightful place in the Church in Australia and being a part of fulfilling the destiny of this Great Southland. These words have largely been from Non-Indigenous prophetic voices.

Katie Dunstan, in her book 'Ancient Keys to a New Sound – Rising from the Land' is being used by God as a spearhead to break ground as a First Nation Prophet to the Nation, as she takes her place as a Christian Indigenous leader, with a vital contribution to the life of the Church here in Australia and abroad. I believe this book is a prophetic sign of the significant shift in the spirit realm over this nation and the nations in this new era, as it makes way for other Indigenous prophetic voices of the land to come through.

Timothy, my child, I'm giving you these instructions based on the prophecies that were once made concerning you. So if you follow them, you can wage a good warfare because you have faith and a good conscience. (1 Timothy 1:18-19)

There are many prophecies made concerning Australian Aboriginals and Torres Strait Islanders Christians that have been fulfilled, but there is yet much more to be fulfilled, especially in the areas of full recognition of spiritual authority in the anointing of the five-fold ministry gifts God has ordained for His Church in Australia. Katie is a part of the greater outworking of this, as she walks in greater Spiritual authority in the five-fold anointing and prophetic mantle she has for this nation. She has, in many cases, lived the prophetic revelation in this book, as prophets often do.

Myself and many other Australian Indigenous Christian Leaders have acted on the prophetic words spoken over our ministries and have had the faith and good conscience to fight the good fight against the unrecognised and uncredited contributions we've made to the Church in Australia over generations.

Katie and her book is fulfilment of generations of prayer and intercession for the five-fold prophetic to come forth through our people and be recognised and valued as a gift to the body of Christ.

Recognition of the five-fold ministry gifts of Apostles, Prophets, Evangelists, Pastors and Teachers among the Australian Indigenous Christian Leaders needs to be given ample opportunities in the wider Australian Christian Church to development and deliver what God has ordained for this current time and season.

For a long time the church has been operating with three of the 5 fold in the body; namely the Pastor, Evangelist and Teacher. But it's great to be seeing, even at this time, a day that we've been waiting for, that is the release of the prophetic and apostolic. Katie, in her book provides us with a powerful compilation of prophetic words, strategies, prayers, decrees and direction for Australia, the Great South Lands of the Holy Spirit and many nations to enter into greater fullness of their destiny. I thank God that Katie has heard from God and responded to complete this assignment to write and release this prophetic blueprint for this new era. She has embarked on a mission to build a foundation and raise up the prophetic voice here in our land, and the Great Southland of the Holy Spirit, and especially amongst our Indigenous peoples.

The prophetic, I know has not been strange to our Indigenous peoples, because God has somehow built within us the sense of being able to discern and see things in the Spirit, and often before it even happens. I believe Katie has discerned the times and seasons and is sharing it for you to partner with it, to see God's will done here in our lands as it is in heaven.

I remember some years ago having an in depth conversation with John Dawson, former International President for Youth With A Mission and (author of "Taking our Cities for God" also "Healing America's Wounds"). We spoke in regards to the powerful prophetic insight of Indigenous Christians from around the world especially the high spiritual level of discernment, words of wisdom and words of knowledge that unlocked kingdom mysteries over the land and cities to release the destiny of a nation and how we agreed as both Apostolic and Prophetic spiritual Father's the need to champion the prophetic anointing that's on the rising Indigenous Prophets and Apostles in the earth.

I believe God is building His church and, as Katie highlights in her book, God is raising up the five-fold amongst First Nations people across the world. Katie walks in the mantle of a Prophet to the nation and releases a unique contribution that is needed by the broader Body of Christ. Through 'Ancient Keys to a New Sound – Rising from the Land' I believe the Body of Christ will be strengthened to arise into her God given destiny.

Tim Edwards
Australian Indigenous Christian Leader
Apostolic Father to the Nation
Tim Edwards Ministries

Foreword by Jenny Haggar

There are times in God's prophetic timeline for our nation that He breaks through with a significant shift.

Katie Dunstan's book *"Ancient Keys to a New Sound Rising from the Land",* is an exciting revelation of the unlocking and releasing of the First Nation prophetic voice in our land.

"Behold, I will do a new thing, now it shall spring forth, shall you not know it? I will even make a road in the wilderness and rivers in the desert." – Isaiah 43:19 (NKJV)

Without the voice of our First Nation people we are incomplete in our journey as a nation, and especially as they are gifted in discerning of spiritual realities. They have taught me so much in the years that we have at times prayed together, and I have come to understand something of the spiritual battle they face in an attempt to silence them as a people, and stop them rising to their Kingdom destiny.

Katie's book is powerful revelation from the Throne Room as the Father, through her prophetic voice, speaks to us as a nation – Indigenous and non-Indigenous.

A new sound is being released from the land as chains are being broken and lives resurrected; a sound of freedom and new authority to rise and conquer! Dry bones are receiving new life and revelation! Old mindsets are being destroyed! New strategies are being birthed from the Throne Room!

Her book took me back to the time of the British Reconciliation Team's visit to Australia in September 1998, as a result of a divine encounter that happened on a bus on the way to Prayer Mountain in Korea in 1993.

Brian Mills, the father of the prayer movement in the UK, found himself seated next to our First Nation Apostle Tim Edwards, who shared with him some of the dark history of British colonisation in Australia. Brian was shocked at the depth of sin towards Tim's people, hearing among other things that there were 1200 massacre sites recorded throughout Australia. When Brian asked him what should be done, Tim replied 'Get a mob together and come over to Australia and say you're sorry.'

The full impact of that visit is recorded in the book 'Fountains of Tears -Changing Nations Through the Power of Repentance and Forgiveness, written by Brian Mills and Australian team leader Brian Pickering. It is a spiritual and historical account of Britain's repentance of the sins of their nation towards Australia and includes a report of a return visit to Britain in October 1999 by 35 intercessors from Australia, including national First Nation leader Apostle Peter Walker. Time was spent offering forgiveness and releasing the British from the pain and anguish with which they had been burdened.

Back in 1998 when we first heard that 32 British intercessors intended to visit our shores and travel the length and breadth of our nation repenting for the sins of Britain, we did not know what to expect. In advance of their visit, they asked us to look at historical accounts and come up with the major British offenses that they needed to address.

It was a dark history covering many aspects of our colonial past, and more recent events.

After they arrived in South Australia we took the team to the site of the Colebrook Children's Training Home at Eden Hills, where between 1943 and 1972 350 First Nation children of the Stolen Generation were brought down from Oodnadatta and Quorn to go to the school in Adelaide. While all buildings have long gone, there is now a beautiful carved boulder of an Aboriginal woman weeping for her lost children, forming a fountain of tears. We were formally welcomed on the land by our First Nation people who had come to receive the British apology, including elder Mona Olsson who had taught me so much about her people. Mona had a powerful encounter with the Lord in the desert when five years old and she was eventually reconciled with her mother who sadly could not see her because she had lost her sight.

As we began to repent and pray, the anguish of their suffering came upon us. The Holy Spirit fell in such power and began to lead us in deep travail and conviction.

Brian Mills read Jeremiah 31:15 (NJKV)

Thus says the Lord:
"A voice was heard in Ramah, Lamentation and bitter weeping Rachel weeping for her children, Refusing to be comforted for her children, Because they are no more."

Then he began to prophesy - *'They will return from the land of the enemy so there is hope for your future … your children will return to their own land, receive them, welcome them, comfort them, teach them, … Let my love be amongst you to bring that healing.'*

Suddenly I felt the most intense righteous anger come upon me; feeling the full burden of God's heart for these people of the land. I began to prophecy:

My! My! My! They have been in the night so long they can't see the day. You go in there! You go into their pain! You go into their suffering! You go into their poverty. And you release them from it. You break the shackles! You break the chains! For God says 'Those that the Son sets free are free indeed! For not until you go in and not until you do that in My name will I release you in this nation.

I love these people so much I will not bypass them! I will not look the other way! I will not stall, Australia! My hour is coming Australia! My timing is coming Australia! I give you notice, Australia. You lay down your lives and go in there for Me! Into the darkness and though you don't like the darkness, you go in there. You go in there in My name. In My name you lay healing hands! And you go in there and demonstrate my love practically. You don't just demonstrate it in prayer! You demonstrate it in activity. You go in there. You take the anger in My name. You take the bitter root in My name! You take it all in My name because I will strengthen you to do it, says the Lord God.

'Come forth, come forth' says the Lord. 'For I will birth this thing, I will birth this thing in the affliction. I will bring back my Aboriginal children… I will give them the keys of the Kingdom of God. There will be no more shame upon these people! I will come! And I will take the shame from them! And I will give them My robes of righteousness, says the Lord. This is a new day for Australia. The Lord leaves the ninety-nine to go and find the one that is lost… He is leaving us to go and find them and bring them to Himself.'

Brian Mills then prophesied again:

"Unless you do this white Australia, unless you enter into their pain, they will be blessed, and you will be unblessed. But as you enter into their pain, as you go into their anguish, as you begin to identify with them, as you reach out in love, then you will share in the blessings I will pour out on them. But unless you do, you will miss what I want to do…you will miss it! This is strategic, this is My word to you. Hear my heart, "says God. "Hear My heart" says the Father." "Hear my heart."

Until we enter the spiritual battle that our First Nation people face, especially against the spirit of death, it is difficult to fully comprehend these words of the Lord. He was calling us to the Cross - to face the anger and bitterness, deep pain and cry for justice.

To sit in the dirt with the 'aunties' and wail in lamentation for all that had been stolen from them. To look out on the landscape of desolation and know that the only one who can bring deliverance was the Lord God Almighty, and just as He promised, as Katie explains in her excellent insightful book, He is gloriously doing so.

He is breathing into the dry bones, strengthening them to stand on their feet and releasing them as His prophetic voice in the land. They are rising up in the authority He has given them to be overcomers, ruling and reigning with Him.

It is no coincidence that Katie was on a recent Zoom call led by some of the people from Britain who were at the Fountain of Tears that day. The Lord is reminding us of his faithfulness. Her book is part of the fulfilment of all that God promised during that historic visit. God is calling his First Nation people to arise to their destiny, to all He had planned for them before the foundation of the world. A glorious destiny!

Jenny Hagger AM
Director Australian House of Prayer for All Nations.
South Pacific House of Prayer. Mission World Aid.
Lead pastor Father's House in Adelaide.

Introduction:

*Y*aama maliyaa (Yarma maleeyiah) – Hello friends, and welcome to a journey through some prophetic insights into *'Ancient Keys to a New Sound Rising from the Land.'*

These ancient keys will unlock doors to new pathways that have been carved out for the new era that we have entered into. Let's journey together to discover these ancient keys to the new era. I believe they are His keys to the release of the nation.

Let me begin by sharing a little about my personal journey:

I am a Gomeroi murri-yinnar (mu-ree yi-nahr) (Aboriginal woman) from Walhallow (Wol-hollow) Reserve, known as Caroona Mission near the Mooki (Mook-eye) River in North Western NSW. My people are the Gomeroi people. I was the seventh born of eight children to Ivan and Winnie Allen (nee Sampson).

I was radically delivered out of witchcraft through a life changing encounter with Jesus in 1998. While I was training to move through the levels of witchcraft – Jesus turned up – He appeared to me. I was in a vision of a pool, the bottom of the pool was mosaic. In the mosaic tiles Jesus appeared, with arms outstretched to me. He was calling me to Himself. It was a Nathaniel and the fig tree moment. It was like He saw me in this darkness closing in on me to take my soul and Jesus turned up. After being delivered, healed and restored from a life of trauma and turmoil, I now get to partner with Holy Spirit to see Jesus bring life-changing healing and transformation to wounded souls and the hearts of nations, as I travel around our nation of Australia and abroad into South Eastern Asia.

While at Ganggalah Bible College on Bunjalung (Bun-juh-lung) Country Tweed Heads NSW in 2007, I was mentored in the prophetic by a Prophet of the house (Ganggalah Church), who I travelled into South Korea with for 3 years.

I am very grateful to Holy Spirit for speaking to me about aligning with Bruce and Cheryl Lindley who we aligned with a number of years ago, and became part of ARC Global apostolic and prophetic community. From there I was spearheaded into my prophetic calling at an accelerated rate.

From humble beginnings I find myself in places like the residence of the President of Israel as part of a Christian Indigenous Trade Mission; and in Israel at the Garden of Gethsemane encountering Jesus.

The prophetic encounters, visions and insights shared in the pages of this book have been part of my journey with Jesus and my story.

At the rise of 2020 we had crossed over into a new year, and a new era. An era is a fixed point in time from which a series of years is reckoned, a period identified by some prominent characteristic feature (Miriam-Webster dictionary). It is a long and distinct period of history with unique features and characteristics.

Since the beginning of time, before the foundations of the earth, Father has had this era in His heart. Some of the unique features marking this new era are ancient blueprints conceived before time that will be birthed for such a time as this. These ancient blueprints have assigned to them ancient keys. This book, I believe is holding for you 'ancient keys to a new sound - rising from the land'.

I feel like this book was waiting in the heavenlies for me to pen from the ancient of time.

The Lord reminds me, my tongue is the pen of a ready writer Psalm 45:1. The Hebrew is literally "My tongue is the pen of a skilful [inspired] scribe." (TPT footnotes). I release the writings in these pages with a humble and grateful heart, and in reverential fear of the Lord. I am astonished that the Lord has given this assignment to me. My confidence is in Him (See Jerimiah 17:7; 2 Corinthians 7:16) and I am obedient to follow Him where He takes me.

During the time of living through the pages that follow, I spent many hours night and day in deep travail, while pregnant with and birthing the revelation and prophetic insights found within. The process is real!

I must say I thoroughly enjoyed and was in total awe of Jesus during my adventures with Him, and the many exhilarating hours of being in extraordinary encounters and visions with Him. Many times I would be so overcome by His Spirit and glory, deep in His presence that I could hardly move. What fun and an incredible privilege and honour!

This book is a compilation of what I believe to be some of the Ancient keys to the new era. Ancient because I believe each one has been in the heart of the Father since the beginning of time. It has been His original plan for us to use these *Ancient Keys to unlock this New Sound Rising from the Land*'. This sound has been locked up in the land and it is time for it to arise and resound.

In the pages of this book you will find encounters and visions revealing prophetic keys, revelations and strategies to help navigate God's plan for Australia and, I believe, other nations. I believe this is part of the divine strategy to see Australia come into her God given destiny, and nations to come to the brightness of the church's arising in glory light (see Isaiah 60:3).

I believe the keys revealed through this book will play a part to usher in the end time move of God in this nation and the nations.
I believe we will see the greatest move of the Spirit of God across the nations we have ever seen or known before. This book holds some keys to unlock this move.

We see in part, and this is simply the part that I see in a much bigger picture of what God is doing in this new era.

There is an invitation for us all to *go low* in humility, and *go deeper* into the presence of God in the secret place than we have ever been. God is calling us, to then *rise* in high ranking authority, equipped to *release* the living Word of God to set the captives free, release the prisoners from deep darkness, heal the sick, cleanse the lepers, raise the dead and do greater works then He.

The key to this doorway of ancient wisdom, revelation, authority and lightning bolt power is an invitation into a John 17:21-23 oneness, so that we may be one as Jesus is one with the Father. It is an invitation to enter into an unchartered unity, oneness, and family that is yet to manifest amongst us. This oneness encompasses every tongue, tribe and nation (see Revelation 5:9) and I like to include denomination and generation.

While this book is written with prophetic insights for the nation of Australia, I strongly believe it has application and relevance for other nations. I believe it will take the nations to embrace and use such keys to unlock the move of God across the nations in this new era, in a way that makes way for the new sound rising from the land.

At the end of each chapter you will find either key scriptures, prayers, decrees or a combination of these. I encourage you to speak them out loud. The Bible says, 'decree a thing and it will be established' (Job 22:28 NIV).

In the Hebrew calendar we have stepped into the decade of *'pey'. 'Pey '*means *voice* or *mouth*. As ambassadors for Christ, the voice of God through our voices must rise and resound and be heard in this new era.

It is time for the voices that have not been heard to awake and come forth. 'First Nations voices of the land come forth'. We need God's voice through the voices of the diverse people groups in our nation to roar as one sound in one accord.

When we lift our voice and decree what God is saying, it shifts ancient old atmospheres that have impeded the destiny of nations. As we decree the word of God, a divine shift takes place as ancient strongholds are broken off the land and new song-lines of wild worship to the Lord are established across our lands. *Ancient keys to a new sound rising from the land.*

As you come into agreement and decree your way through this book, you will be decreeing our future, a future that unlocks God's kingdom plan for our nation and realigns heaven and earth.

Patricia King in her book 'Decree a thing, and it shall be established, third edition 2012' says: 'The following are some reasons why the confession of the word is found to be powerful in our lives. The word of God: is eternal in the heavens - Matthew 24:35; will not return void - Isaiah 55:11; Frames the will of God - Hebrews 11:3; dispatches angels - Psalm 103:20; brings light into darkness - Psalm 119:130; Is a lamp unto our feet and a light unto our path - Psalm 119:105; secures blessings - Ephesians 1:3; 2 Peter 1:3; is seed - Mark 4; Is our weapon of warfare – Ephesians 6:10-20; 2 Corinthians 10:3-5; pulls down mindsets – 2 Corinthians 10:3-5; creates – Romans 4:17; sanctifies – John 17:17; strengthens the Spirit man Ephesians 5:26; and ensures answers to prayer – John 15:7.

So I encourage you to speak out loud the prayers, decrees and key scriptures highlighted at the end of each chapter, to activate strategies for 'Ancient Keys to the New Era' – A New Sound Rising from the Land. As we partner with Holy Spirit we will see God's will established for our Nation of Australia and the nations. I invite you to pray for, proclaim, declare and decree, travail for and also to partner with the prophetic insights in the pages of this book as Holy Spirit leads you.

Challenge yourself to pick up and run with some of the strategic keys. It is an opportunity to ask ourselves 'how can I partner with these keys in this new era?' Be attuned to what the Spirit is saying to the church. Be attuned to what Holy Spirit is breathing on for you.

I encourage you to prepare your heart to be enlarged as we embark on this journey through these prophetic encounters together. Expect and allow Holy Spirit to *take you* into divine encounters as *you take* this journey.

My heart for you, as you journey through this book, is that you will be open to receive from Holy Spirit. I pray for impartations, downloads, revelations and life changing encounters with Him that mark and change you forever and leave you awe-struck and love-struck for Jesus. My prayer is, that you will encounter Jesus in ways that will empower, challenge and inspire you to join the remnant army of reformers rising from this nation to unite an ignite other nations for the revival fire, reformation and transformation that will mark this era. Let us arise as the glorious diverse and unified Bride that we are and take the nation for Jesus, crowned in Kingdom unity that will release the new sound rising from the land.

Your sister with the same Father

Katie x

Chapter 1

Voices of the Land

42 'And I know that You always hear Me, but because of the people who are standing by I said this, that they may believe that You sent Me." 43 Now when He had said these things, He cried with a loud voice, "Lazarus, **come forth**!" 44 And he who had died came out bound hand and foot with grave clothes, and his face was wrapped with a cloth. Jesus said to them, 'Loose him, and let him go.'

(John 11:42-44 NKJV)

I believe one of the *ancient keys* to the era of revival, reformation and transformation that is beginning to take place, is for our First Nations people, all over the globe, to rise up and take their place as part of the end time global move of God. I sense the Father's heart cheering us all on together, all nations, Indigenous and non-Indigenous as one warrior bride.

In these times I believe the Lord is raising up First Nations people and particularly His voice, through the voice of the First Nations people of Australia and other nations around the globe. A First Nations sound is rising up from the land and filling the atmosphere to shift the atmosphere over the nations.

I am speaking about the voices of the First Nation five-fold Apostles, Prophets, Evangelists, Teachers and Pastors (1); warriors across the seven Spiritual mountains of influence Government, Education, Business, Media, Arts, Family, and Religion (2); and our Intercessors, watchman and gatekeepers (3) and every First Nations Ambassador of heaven's voice. These are all areas that need the voice and wisdom of God through our First Nations people.

First Nations people, we need your voice. Your nation needs your voice. Your voice is an *ancient key* to the end time revival fires that the Lord wants to use to set nations ablaze. Partnering with the Lord in this will be an important part of reforming the church as a whole, and part of the transformation that is about to take place. Steward your voice for the Kingdom of God well.

Honouring our Elders and Christian Forefathers

I would like to take time here to honour our Christian Elders and leaders that have walked this road and fought this fight, laying down their lives to see our people begin to arise and be all we are called to be, for the glory of the Lord.
This, I believe is another *ancient key* to usher in the end time move of God.

Many, many of our First Nations Fathers and Mothers have lived and moved and had their being in God. They have lived a life of being led by Holy Spirit, as they have given their all to partner with the Lord, and carve out the road ahead for us and the generations to come. I do not take lightly the years and lifetime of struggle and triumph they have been through, and just what that means for us today, and for the future. This generational sowing and reaping is evident in our lives today. So thank you from my heart. Your sacrifice is acknowledged and you are honoured. Our God is the same yesterday, today and forever. We have an awesome future. All glory and all honour to God.

God says:

For I know the plans I have for you, declares the Lord, plans to prosper you, and not to harm you, plans to give you hope and a future (Jeremiah 29:11 NIV).

This future is supernatural, it's more than we could ever imagine or hope for.

Now to Him who is able to do exceedingly abundantly above all that we ask or think, according to the power that works in us (Ephesians 3:20 NKJV)

The Lord God Almighty's power is at work in you *'warrior Son,'* and in you *'Daughter of Destiny.'* Raise your voice and glorify the King of Kings and the Lord of Lords. Release the roar of the Lion of the Tribe of Judah that is within you.

One night, I was just falling off to sleep and I began to hear a sound in the Spirit. It was the sound of clapsticks and the digeridoo playing a compilation of raw worship to the Lord.
It was surrounded by sheer abandoned love for the Holy One, the Anointed One, Jesus Christ our Lord. These instruments were accompanied by many First Nations voices of the land, along with a myriad of angels as they all worshipped the Lord together.

My Encounter with God's Heart for Our People

He is for us and not against us!

As I rested at night ready to go to go off to sleep, the Lord took me up into an encounter. We were looking down on our nation of Australia.

I could see what looked like glory mist, rising up from the land, all across our nation. I was in awe. I could sense the intense love of Father God beaming into Australia.

As my eyes zoomed in closer to the land, in the midst of the glory I could see people dancing, and I heard a glorious sound. It was the First Nations people of the land, dancing, cultural way, dust of the land spraying up as their feet hit the ground. The Lords glory was released into the land as they stomped in the dance. The land around their feet became filled with the glory. The more they danced, the more the glory increased and filled the atmosphere.

> *Then people everywhere will know about the Glory of the LORD. This news will spread just as water spreads out into the sea* (Habakkuk 2:14 ERV)

> *But the earth will be as full of the knowledge of the LORD's glory as the seas are full of water* (Habakkuk 2:14 GNT)

> *Then people everywhere will know the Lord's greatness. This news will spread like water covering the sea* (Habakkuk 2:14 ICB)

I was reminded of Ruth Heflin's Book "Glory- Experiencing the Atmosphere of Heaven" where she writes, "dance brings an anointing for the nations"(P27). Reflecting on David dancing before the Lord with all his might as he brought the Ark of the Lord into Jerusalem she writes "if we want to bring in the Ark of God we would have to dance too (p24). What she was saying was, dancing releases the Glory of God (the Ark of God) and brings an anointing for nations. (4)

What I saw was more than just a great joyful celebration, but the glory of the Lord being released into the land through the stomp in the dance.

As I watched on, I could see the glory spreading. It filled the land of our nation, like the knowledge of the glory of the Lord that fills the earth.

The First Nations people carry a glory that is unique to them/us. This glory is yet to be released into the nations and I believe it is a powerful *ancient key* to unlock the glory sound of God in the nations. I believe we are entering the times for this glory to spill out. As we walk together, this sound will arise, this glory will manifest.

The sense I had was that these First Nation Countrymen and women were dancing to the rhythm of an *'ancient love'* that compelled them to *'arise and dance'* with song. An ancient love that wooed them and drew them back to their first love - Jesus.

> *Break forth with dancing! Make music and sing God's praises with the rhythm of the drums. 4 For he enjoys his faithful lovers. He adorns the humble with his beauty and he loves to give them the victory.* (Psalm 149:3-4 TPT)

> *We love him, because he first loved us* (1 John 4:19 KJV)

The victory that is about to become reality will spread across the nations and is rooted in first love.

This ancient love seemed to rise from deep within the age old layers of this beautiful land. As this happened, it felt to me, like an intergenerational love for our Creator was drawn from an ancient timeline, up through the feet of the First Nations people, and released into the now timeline. It was released through their dance, their song, their hands, and as we all join hands and hearts, the love of God becomes known through our lives in the present day. We will be known by the fruit of this ancient love of God; the one who loved us before the foundations of the earth. This intergenerational, ancient love was *re-ignited* within the people. It brought with it a timeless refreshing.

This whole encounter was surrounded with a strong sense of being surrendered and positioned right in the centre of a place that beckons *draw near to me and I will draw near to you* (see James 4:8). This is a place of habitation in the secret place, where our heart is in a constant state of consuming love, pursuing God's heart.

Let us run to draw near to Him and hang out with Jesus, in His presence for as long, and as often as we can. Let us not only pursue His presence, but let us pursue the Father's heart
To know His heart so intimately and in such fullness that we swell with the goodness of the Father and become His heartbeat in the land. Let us begin to move to the rhythm of the sound that is resounding across the land. It is the rhythm of the Fathers heartbeat, for in Him we live and move and have our being.

> [28] *'For in him we live and move and have our being.' As some of your own poets have said, 'We are his offspring.'* (Acts 17:28 NIV)

I heard in the Spirit:

'She is lit with love'

The hearts of the First Nations people were lit up with love for Jesus!

As the perfect love of God poured out through the land and through the people, the sheer power of this pure love caused ancient strongholds to be broken off the land and off the people. The land itself was breaking free from shackles and being saturated and soaked in the love and the pure goodness of God.

As this perfect love of God was poured and moved throughout the landscape, First Nations people were the treasures being unearthed from the lower layers of the land.

The love of God was washing away all reproach and revealing these priceless treasures. Once hidden, now will be lifted from the miry clay to *decree and declare* the word of the Lord and to display His splendour.

> *¹ I waited patiently and expectantly for the Lord; and He inclined to me and heard my cry.*
>
> *² He drew me up out of a horrible pit [a pit of tumult and of destruction], out of the miry clay (froth and slime), and set my feet upon a rock, steadying my steps and establishing my goings.*
>
> *³ And He has put a new song in my mouth, a song of praise to our God. Many shall see and fear (revere and worship) and put their trust and confident reliance in the Lord* (Psalm 40:1-3 AMP)

I just love how the Amplified version translates this verse: 'many shall see and fear, revere and worship and put their trust and confident reliance in the Lord'! What other state of being would you want to be positioned in? Then the word goes on in the book of Isaiah to outline these promises:

> *… and provide for those who grieve in Zion— to bestow on them a crown of beauty instead of ashes, the oil of joy instead of mourning, and a garment of praise instead of a spirit of despair. They will be called oaks of righteousness, a planting of the* LORD *for the **display** of his **splendour**.* (Isaiah 61:3 NIV) *emphasis is mine.*

The whole chapter of Isaiah 61 is stunning! I encourage you to meditate on it, focussing on Jesus as you do.

I believe the Lord is unearthing His hidden treasures. Those hidden treasures are the First Nations voices of the Land, causing them to *arise* and *resound*, no longer *bound*! Hallelujah, what joy there is on that right there friends!

I want to decree right here:

'First Nations people, the joy of the Lord is your strength!'
'You are Gods treasure'

'Arise and resound, arise and let God's voice be heard.'

'Let the voice and word of the Lord shoot forth from your mouth like the sword of the Lord that it is.'

What I was seeing was, the First Nations Sons and Daughters arising from the land with a *dance of deliverance* and a *strong song* - with a *new voice*.

> *O God, my saving God, deliver me fully from every sin, even the sin that brought bloodguilt. Then my heart will once again be thrilled to sing the passionate songs of joy and **deliverance**!* (Psalm 51:14 TPT) *emphasis is mine.*

From the land, a new sound surrounded me. Immediately I felt and sensed the dry bones in the land of Australia. The dry bones represented the people of the land who previously had no voice. God is coming to unlock and unblock the stopped-up prison doors, to cause your voice to run free in the Spirit of the Lord, declaring and decreeing His truth in the land.

I decree *unlock and release*, *unlock and release, unlock and release,* in Jesus name. Where the spirit of the Lord is, there is freedom. The Spirit of the Lord is upon us, we are free!! Amen!

Ezekiel 37:1-14 The Valley of Dry Bones (NIV)

37 *The hand of the* LORD *was on me, and he brought me out by the Spirit of the* LORD *and set me in the middle of a valley; it was full of bones.*

2 He led me back and forth among them, and I saw a great many bones on the floor of the valley, bones that were very dry. 3 He asked me, "Son of man, can these bones live?"

I said, "Sovereign LORD*, you alone know."*

4 Then he said to me, "Prophesy to these bones and say to them, 'Dry bones, hear the word of the LORD*!*

5 This is what the Sovereign LORD *says to these bones: I will make breath enter you, and you will come to life.*

6 I will attach tendons to you and make flesh come upon you and cover you with skin; I will put breath in you, and you will come to life. Then you will know that I am the LORD*.'"*

7 So I prophesied as I was commanded. And as I was prophesying, there was a noise, a rattling sound, and the bones came together, bone to bone. 8 I looked, and tendons and flesh appeared on them and skin covered them, but there was no breath in them.

9 Then he said to me, "Prophesy to the breath; prophesy, son of man, and say to it, 'this is what the Sovereign LORD *says: Come, breath, from the four winds and breathe into these slain, that they may live.'" 10 So I prophesied as he commanded me, and breath entered them; they came to life and stood up on their feet—a vast army.*

[11] Then he said to me: "Son of man, these bones are the people of Israel. They say, 'Our bones are dried up and our hope is gone; we are cut off.'

[12] Therefore prophesy and say to them: 'this is what the Sovereign LORD says: My people, I am going to open your graves and bring you up from them; I will bring you back to the land of Israel.

*[13] Then you, my people, will know that I am the LORD, when I open your graves and bring you up from them. [14] **I will put my Spirit in you and you will live, and I will settle you in your own land**. Then you will know that I the LORD have spoken, and I have done it, declares the LORD.'* (NIV)

I prophesy to these bone – live! I prophesy to these dry bones, hear the word of God. I prophesy you bones are no longer dried up, you bones are revived and full of life. I decree your hope is restored and it is contagious. I prophesy you are not cut off but you are securely grafted-in to the King of Kings.

I prophesy come, breath of God come, from the four winds, from the North, the South, the East and the West and breathe the breath of God into these bones. I prophesy life to these bones - yes you will live. I prophesy to the bones of the First Nations people, across this earth – live! I prophesy First Nations people, across the earth, you will stand up on your feet, you are the vast army of the Lord, in Jesus mighty name. The Spirit of God is put within you and you are settled in your own land. Amen!

Lyrics from this song called RATTLE! By Elevation Worship (5) resonates so powerfully through my bones right now. See RATTLE! | Official Lyric Video | Elevation Worship:

This is the sound
Of the dry bones rattling

This is the praise
Make a dead man walk again
Open the grave I'm coming out
I'm gonna live
Gonna live again
This is the sound
Of the dry bones rattling!

And then it goes on to decree:

LIVE! LIVE!
Dry bones hear the word of the Lord!

I speak to the dry bones of the First Nations people of the Land and I decree: LIVE! LIVE! Dry bones Hear the word of the Lord and LIVE!

A New Sound: New Song Lines

There was a *new sound* coming from the First Nations bones. It was a mighty and awesome sound rattling and resounding throughout the land, with power to set the captives *free*. The sound came forth as the bones came forth, and as the people came forth from graves in the ground.

The sound of the First Nations People arising is a declaration to the enemy - *'no more.'* No more killing, no more stealing joy and life, no more destroying destinies. *'No More, No More'* proclaimed the beat of the clap sticks that resound through the generational timelines. The decree of the song was reinforced by the stomping rhythm of the feet as our First Nations people danced on the red dust soil. Life was rising and released through the feet stomping to the rhythm of the decree.

As they danced a *canopy of worship* shot up like a parachute covering the nation.

The worship caused a *re-wiring* and *releasing* of *new song-lines of wild worship* throughout our land. Song-lines declaring *life and freedom*. Song lines forged by the Spirit of the Lord, for where the Spirit of the Lord is there is freedom.

> [16] *But whenever anyone turns to the Lord, the veil is taken away.* [17] *Now the Lord is the Spirit, and where the Spirit of the Lord is, there is freedom.*
> [18] *And we all, who with unveiled faces contemplate*[a] *the Lord's glory, are being transformed into his image with ever-increasing glory, which comes from the Lord, who is the Spirit.* (2 Corinthians 3:16-18 NIV)

As we unveil faces and take off the mask of who we think we have to be, we are being transformed from glory to glory!

What are Song Lines?

Song-lines are the Aboriginal walking routes that crossed the country, linking important sites and locations. The term 'song-line' describes the features and directions of travel that were included in a song that was sung and memorised for the traveller to know the route to their destination.

Song-lines contain information about the land and how the traveller should respectfully make their trip. This includes the types of food that were safe to eat, places to be avoided and the boundaries of each Mob's (people groups) Country that the traveller could pass through.

Song-lines also describe features and landmarks that the traveller should look out for so they knew that they are going in the right direction. Other examples of 'signposts' or 'markers' include rock formations, bends in rivers, or trees with naturally forming spirals, or arches.

A Cultural Passport:

One example of a Song-line is the 3,500km travel route that connected the central desert region with the eastern coast of the country (modern day Byron Bay).

This particular travel route allowed the desert communities to visit the ocean where they could witness how dolphins were used by the people to heard fish. Similarly people from the coastal communities were able to travel and visit the culturally important sites of Uluru and other places.

Song-lines also act as a 'Cultural Passport' when travelling through the country of another Mob. The verses that relate to a particular region, can be sung in the local language so that the people living there know that travellers are passing through in a respectful manner.

(source: deadlystory.com) (6)

Song-lines Redeemed as the Streams of Living Waters

Jesus, the way-maker makes a way for these ancient song-lines throughout the land to be restored to its full intent in God, by compelling our First Nations people to see and encounter Jesus along the road. To know God, the one true living God:

To acknowledge Creator God in creation in a more profound way, in the land marks, at the gathering places. Streams of living waters rise up from the underground water ways. Streams rise up through the land, and through the people. As we sing our way through the route, the pathway, the road-map, we will be singing to Jesus and be singing about God's creation of river-ways, waterways, rock formations and landmarks. We will be worshipping Jesus and acknowledging and honouring Jesus for creating heaven and earth and for making a way to travel across the land in our nation.

We will be worshipping Jesus for guiding our steps along the journey. It speaks to me of *'song-lines redeemed as streams of living waters.'*

Now our people can travel the land carrying the life giving water of the living word of God. As we stop and gather, worship and feed on the word of God, we can drink deeply of Him. As we worship, we create these new song-lines, redeemed as the streams of living waters. These new song-lines open up a new way to share and grow together in the nature, character and the ways of God. For His ways are not our ways, His ways are higher.

Our cultural way of moving through the song-lines is still intact, and now it is the power of the blood of Jesus that flows through every song-line. We will see that God has restored this beautiful cultural practice to the fullness of His original intent for the song-lines of our nation. Restored to all they were destined to be before the beginning of time, for people to travel along and to stop, to gather and to worship.
To worship and glorify the one true living God, in the landscapes and walking routes, in the desert lands, coastlands and in-lands, in the mountains, in the river-ways, and across the airways. Oh glory to your name Lord Jesus!

With this re-establishing of Gods original intent, that is for Jesus to be the centre of it all, our people are released to share ancient wisdom and revelation like we have not seen. The song-lines travelled create an open heaven over the nation. The tracks across the land ways become like rivers of glory filling the land. As the tracks and pathways are carved out, powerful portals of glory are opened, for the glory of the Lord to flow through and be released in our lands along with the knowledge of the glory of the Lord as it begins to cover the earth as the waters cover the sea (see Habakkuk 2:14).

In my encounter I believe this is the glory mist that I see arising across our nation, released as our First Nations people stomp the ground as they dance.

What an incredibly loving God we serve, He loves all people and He loves our First Nations people all over the world. He is honouring us in our cultural practices that line-up with the word of God. He is restoring His original purpose and intent within our cultural practices to enrich and bring our nation into the fullness and glory of God. The power of the Spirit of God is moving mightily across the landscape and waterways of our nation. Where the Spirit of the Lord is, there is freedom. He is setting our nation free and restoring it to Himself to lift her up and to display His splendour through our nation, to all the nations.

Come Forth!

Just as Lazarus responded to the voice of Jesus calling 'Lazarus come forth'. These bones in my encounter represented the sound of the First Nations voices responding to the call of the Father to *'come forth.'* The voices carried a message of *'resurrection life'* and *'life abundant'* to be released into the atmosphere and loosed over our land Australia, in a way that's never been heard, and that's never been seen before.

[41] So they took away the stone. Then Jesus looked up and said, "Father, I thank you that you have heard me.

11:41 TPT Footnote: Resurrection power is released when we give thanks to God. Jesus stood at Lazarus' tomb and gave thanks, then commanded him to arise. Giving thanks to God has more power than you can ever imagine.

> *⁴² And I know that You always hear Me, but because of the people who are standing by I said this, that they may believe that You sent Me." ⁴³ Now when He had said these things, He cried with a loud voice,* **"Lazarus, come forth!"** *⁴⁴ And he who had died came out bound hand and foot with graveclothes, and his face was wrapped with a cloth. Jesus said to them, "Loose him, and let him go."* (John 11:42-44 NKJV) *emphasis is mine.*

I believe we are in a John 11:43 Lazarus time where Jesus is calling our First Nations people, right here in Australia and abroad, to *come forth* and be loosed from your graveclothes. Your hands and feet are no longer bound but free. Remove your graveclothes and come forth in the resurrection power of Jesus Christ, by the power of the blood of Jesus and in the name of Jesus!

A New Stream of First Nations Messengers Activated and Anointed

I believe the Lord is *re-shaping* the face of the land and *Re-setting* the foundation of old to *reveal* the *found nation of now*. The Lord is calling out the original, *divine destiny* for the First Nations people of Australia and the nations, to take their place as part of a bride being fashioned without spot, wrinkle or blemish. He is calling them forth to take their place as part of the remnant army arising. The declaration over Australia – Australia you are a *found nation*! You are not lost to the Kingdom of darkness, you are found and part of the Kingdom army of the Lord marked for a mighty purpose.

Right here I knew Father had His eyes of desire fixed on His bride at this time, and I felt His heart pounding in anticipation for the revealing of the First Nation Sons of God in these times.

There is coming an unveiling of a greater part of the Bride of Christ that will exquisitely know and honour the First Nations people groups and the significance of their role in the awakening of this nation in this hour.

We will begin to hear their voices, for the Lord is *popping open*, what were in times past, deaf ears to hear what the Spirit is saying in the present for our future – by and through His First Nations people.

The Lord will release a new sound, a strong song, a new voice.

A new stream of First Nations messengers, from Australia and from around the world, are being *activated* and *anointed* for such a time as this. It's time! It's time! We will begin to hear the Voices of the First Nations people of the Land join their voices with our Non-Indigenous voices. This powerful uniting as one voice will command blessing over our nation, and over your nation. It can't help but bring increase and new dimensions of *freedom* and *flourishing* to our nation, and nations.

It will prepare the way to usher in the coming end time Revival and Awakening to the Great Southlands of the Holy Spirit and to all the nations of the earth.

The Angel Armies are on the Job

Right after this encounter, I felt led to take up my shofar and I walked outside onto my back veranda. I lifted my shofar and sounded it three times.

At the first sound: in the Spirit realm I saw the sky fill with angel armies, filing into line.

At the second sound: those angel armies swiftly flew in, took their place right in front of me and saluted to the Commander of the Lord of Hosts, Jesus.

At the third sound: off they flew. As quickly as they assembled, they were dispatched.

I knew in my Spirit, they had just taken their orders from Jesus and were armed with a battle strategy, assigned to see the word of the Lord accomplished.

I was astonished and astounded by what just took place. It left me in total awe of God.

Listen for it, can you hear the new sound rising from the land? Watch for the new style of bridal dance. Open your heart to encounter a new dimension of love that is not stopped up. For He is unstopping the wells of free flowing, ancient, eternal love that spans the ages, the generations, the timelines and the nations.
Let me encourage you to get on board with what the Lord is doing in this hour, in this new era. Join hearts, join hands, and lock shields with His First Nations warriors, as the army of the Lord. First Nations and Non-Indigenous together will all arise to take this nation and the nations for Jesus.

Decree with me:

In Jesus name:

I decree, Voices of the Land *arise* and *resound*! In Jesus name Amen!

First Nations people, I decree, now come forth. You are loosed from your graveclothes. (See John 11:42-44 NKJV)

I decree, First Nations people, come forth and live, your hands and feet are no longer bound. Your hands and feet have been set free to lead, with Christ. (See John 11:42-44 NKJV)

First Nations people, I decree that the shackles are now broken off you.

I decree that your future is full of hope, it is filled with exceedingly abundantly more than you could ever ask or think. (See Jerimiah 29:11 NIV and Ephesians 3:20).

I decree that the power of God Almighty is at work in you. (See Ephesians 3:20 NKJV)

I decree, First Nations people break forth with dancing worship to the Lord. (See Psalm 149:3-4 TPT)

I decree that you are His faithful lovers. (See Psalm 149:3-4 TPT)

I decree that the Lord loves to give you victory. He has adorned you with His beauty. (See Psalm 149:3-4 TPT)
I decree He loved me first and because of this I am able to truly love you Jesus. (See 1 John 4:19 KJV)

I decree you are lit with love for Jesus Christ and the light of Christ in you will draw an end time harvest to Jesus.

I decree the Lord has heard your cry, first Nations people. (See Psalm 40:1-3 AMP)

I decree you are lifted out of the pit of destruction, your feet are set upon the rock of Jesus and He has established your goings. (See Psalm 40:1-3 AMP)

I decree the Lord has put a new song of praise to the one true living God in your mouth. You have now put your trust and confident reliance in the Lord God Almighty. You see Him, you revere Him and you worship Him alone. (See Psalm 40:1-3 AMP)

I decree that you are crowned with beauty, the oil of joy is yours, and a garment of praise is what you wear. I decree you are oaks of righteousness, a planting of the Lord and you display His splendour in all its glory. (See Isaiah 61:3 NIV)

I decree you are now fully delivered from every bloodguilt sin and all sin. (See Psalm 51:14 TPT)

I decree your heart is thrilled to sing the passionate songs of deliverance to the Lord. (See Psalm 51:14 TPT)

I decree, turn to the Lord. I decree hear the word of the Lord

I decree the Spirit of the Lord lives inside of you. Where the Spirit of the Lord is, there is freedom. I decree freedom and release over you in Jesus name. I decree that you are being transformed into His image, with ever-increasing glory. (See 2 Corinthians 3:16-18 NIV)

I decree you are loosed, you are set free and I call you to come forth in Jesus name. (See John 11:42-44 NKJV)
I decree that you are seated at the right hand of the Father. Take your rightful place to rule and reign with Christ

Army of the Lord arise and govern the earth as the Ambassadors of the King of Kings that you are.

I decree all of this in the mighty name of Jesus Christ! Amen!

Bible Scriptures used for decrees:

For I know the plans I have for you, plans to prosper you, and not to harm you, but to give you hope and a future (Jerimiah 29:11 NIV).

Now to Him who is able to do exceedingly abundantly above all that we ask or think, according to the power that works in us (Ephesians 3:20 NKJV)

For the knowledge of the glory of God will cover the earth as the waters cover the sea (Habakkuk 2:14)

Break forth with dancing! Make music and sing God's praises with the rhythm of the drums. 4 For he enjoys his faithful lovers. He adorns the humble with his beauty and he loves to give them the victory. (Psalm 149:3&4 TPT)

We love him, because he first loved us (1 John 4:19 KJV)

[1] I waited patiently and expectantly for the Lord; and He inclined to me and heard my cry. [2] He drew me up out of a horrible pit [a pit of tumult and of destruction], out of the miry clay (froth and slime), and set my feet upon a rock, steadying my steps and establishing my goings. [3] And He has put a new song in my mouth, a song of praise to our God. Many shall see and fear (revere and worship) and put their trust and confident reliance in the Lord (Psalm 40:1-3 AMP)

*… and provide for those who grieve in Zion— to bestow on them a crown of beauty instead of ashes, the oil of joy instead of mourning, and a garment of praise instead of a spirit of despair. They will be called oaks of righteousness, a planting of the LORD for the **display** of his **splendour**.* (Isaiah 61:3 NIV)

*O God, my saving God, deliver me fully from every sin, even the sin that brought bloodguilt. Then my heart will once again be thrilled to sing the passionate songs of joy and **deliverance***! (Psalm 51:14 TPT)

[16] *But whenever anyone turns to the Lord, the veil is taken away.* [17] *Now the Lord is the Spirit, and where the Spirit of the Lord is, there is freedom.* [18] *And we all, who with unveiled faces contemplate[a] the Lord's glory, are being transformed into his image with ever-increasing glory, which comes from the Lord, who is the Spirit.* (2 Corinthians 3:16-18 NIV)

[42] *And I know that You always hear Me, but because of the people who are standing by I said this, that they may believe that You sent Me."* [43] *Now when He had said these things, He cried with a loud voice, **"Lazarus, come forth!"*** [44] *And he who had died came out bound hand and foot with graveclothes, and his face was wrapped with a cloth. Jesus said to them, "Loose him, and let him go."* (John 11:42-44 NKJV)

Footnotes:

(1) God is restoring to the church the gifts of the Apostle, Prophet, Evangelist, Pastor and Teacher, also known as the 5 fold. These gifts according to Ephesians 4:12 are given by God to the church to equip the saints for the work of ministry.

(2) God is emphasising to the church the nature and power of the Kingdom of God. God rules over all, and His Kingdom is over all, encompassing every sphere of human life. The revelation of the 7 mountains, taken from Isaiah 2:2 is a recognition that there are 7 spheres of human life that shape the thinking and culture we live in. These include: Government, Education, Business, Media, Arts, Family, and Religion. As the Body of Christ, called to bring heaven to earth, we are commanded to disciple nations by influencing and transforming these mountains of influence

(3) Intercessors, watchman and gatekeepers are those called by God to watch and pray for individuals, families, cities and nations. (Ezekiel 33:1,2,6,7)

(4) Ruth Heflin "Glory- Experiencing the Atmosphere of Heaven" (p24, p27)

(5) RATTLE! (Live) Written by Stephen Furtick, Chris Brown, Brandon Lake 2020 Music by Elevation Worship Publishing, Bethel Music Publishing / Maverick City Publishing Worldwide

(6) source: deadlystory.com

Chapter 2

Tiddas Arise!

"Who is this woman? She is like the sunrise in
all of its glory. She is as beautiful as the moon.
She is as bright as the sun. She is as majestic
as the stars travelling across the sky"

(Song of Songs 6:10 NIRV)

*M*y Spirit soars as I pen this chapter. This is very close to my heart as a First Nations Tidda (Tid-duh) and daughter of the King. Simply writing this book has caused me, as a Tidda, to step-up out of my comfort zone, to arise and run for Jesus in a new way that I have never ran before. The depth of His love for us just astounds and excites me.

During January 2020, the Lord downloaded a prophetic word to me for First Nations women, in Australia and I believe it has magnificent application to First Nations women in all countries. Since then I have gained even more prophetic insight, as the Lord kept unfolding revelation to me.

We had packed up the house, set out in our caravan to take our Breakfree Australia ministry of "Healing Wounded Hearts" and "Sons Arise" on the road and out into our nation of Australia. We set up camp in Far North Queensland for a couple of months, to springboard from there to reach the surrounding areas. We ministered from our books called "Healing Wounded Hearts – Holy Spirit Directed Inner Healing' (1) and "Divine Union" (2). Together with fresh revelation from the Lord, He moved through us to bring healing and deliverance to many people. We have seen so many step into their calling, assignments and destiny, and realise their authority as Sons and Daughters of the King, seated at the right hand of the Father co-ruling and reigning with Christ! What a privilege.

We would often go to a particular spot for a morning, an afternoon or a day, when we weren't ministering. This day, we were there worshipping and praying. I sat on my camp chair in the sand, meditating on my Lord Jesus and the wonder of His goodness.

There I was at the beach, and the tide was coming in, when I heard the Lord say:

'The tide is rising'! Then I heard Him say 'The tide of the Tiddas is rising'

Definition of the word TIDDA:

"TIDDA" (Tid-duh) is a meaningful word used amongst many of Australia's First Nations communities, referring to our women. It means Sister or Sis, but it is so much richer than those words alone. This word "Tidda" is so endearing and is used between many First Nation tribes and languages, permeating geographical and tribal boundaries. It embodies love, honour and respect for that female person.

I would like to take a moment from the outset of this chapter to set the scene and identify that this word has a message for all people, black, white or brindle. I would like to say that this chapter has a First Nations focus, but it has a message for all nations black and white. To see revival fires burn in the Great Southland of the Holy Spirit and across the globe, we need the Tiddas (Tid-duhs) to arise and take their rightful place in the army of God, right alongside our treasured Non-Indigenous sons and daughters of the King.

Also, while I write this mainly from the perspective of First Nation Australian Tiddas, I strongly believe this word is for all First Nation women in many other nations. This word is speaking to you. So if you are a Tidda from the South Pacific Islands Melanesian, Polynesian, Micronesian, Fijian, Samoan, Maori, or Indigenous to your Country, wherever it may be geographically located, this is for you. I encourage you to take it by faith.

I heard the Lord say:

It is time for the TIDDAS to rise and break forth like the dawning of a new day. I am bringing through them waves of fresh wisdom and revelation, and waves of new ways and new strategies.

A New Thing

I feel the heart of God is full with desire to do a new thing through His First Nation women in this new era. What He is doing will release a new level of wisdom and revelation, new ways of doing things, new prayer strategies and new Kingdom strategies to unlock ancient old prison doors and unblock the ancient wells of wisdom that have been blocked up for too long. Tiddas you will set people free with songs of deliverance and release the wells of revival in this land, and in your lands. Your rise will be part of transforming the church and significant in the reformation of society.

> *I am doing something brand new, something unheard of. Even now it sprouts and grows and matures. Don't you perceive it? I will make a way in the wilderness   and open up flowing streams in the desert.* (Isaiah 43:19 TPT)

God is doing a new thing. That means it's not going to look like it has been. It will be new and different, not like it was. So open your heart to receive the new thing the Lord is doing in this hour. It has a sudden surprise element to it. So much so, that it will make a way in what seems like desolate hard ground like the wilderness. But God! Things you thought could never change will flourish. God is all powerful to cause what looks dry and dead to be resurrected in power, just as He opens up the desert ground with streams of living water.

We see an example of this in the book of Isaiah and in Ezekiel:

Isaiah, in referring to the new thing, pictures rivers flowing in the wilderness. The deserts in Israel are typically sandy and arid, with little growing there. However in the layers of the sand lie dormant seeds and small organisms. When the water comes these seeds germinate and come to life. The small organisms also come to life. The rivers turn desolate desert into a spectacular picture of flowers, grass, small bushes and birds. The birds come to feed on the grass seed and the organisms that have come to life.

The prophet with this picture in mind says, "even now it sprouts, and grows and matures, don't you perceive it" God is saying "Things you thought could never change will flourish". God is all powerful to cause what looks dry and dead to be resurrected in power.

The prophet Ezekiel (see Ezekiel 37) was shown a valley with dead, dry, bleached bones scattered throughout it. It's hard to imagine a situation more devoid of life.

Then Ezekiel was commanded to, "Prophesy to these bones and say to them, 'Dry bones, hear the word of the LORD! (v4) So Ezekiel prophesied as he was commanded. As he did, there was a noise, a rattling sound, and the bones came together, bone to bone. He looked, and tendons and flesh appeared on them and skin covered them, but there was no breath in them (v7, 8). Then God said, "Prophesy to the breath; prophesy, son of man, and say to it, 'this is what the Sovereign LORD says: Come, breath, from the four winds and breathe into these slain, that they may live."

So Ezekiel prophesied as he was commanded and breath entered them; they came to life and stood up on their feet—a vast army. (v9)

God can take the dryness of the desert, and a valley of lifeless dry bleached bones and breath on them new life.

I invite you to decree with me:

We speak to the dry bones in this land and we say, awake and arise! We speak to the dry places in the lives of our people, our communities, our nation, and we decree, dry places come to life! You will live and not die!

Tidda, your nation needs you! Tiddas here in Australia, our nation needs your voice, your ancient wisdom, your revelation from the secret place with the Lord. Our nation needs you to arise and shine (see Isaiah 60:1). It's your time to be bold and very courageous (see Joshua 1:6, 7, 9). The Lord is about to do a new thing *in* and *through* you that will impact your life, your families, your extended families, your communities and for some, our nation, in this era.

The Tiddas are carriers of a new song, a new sound. Tidda, you are empowered by the Spirit of God to create new tracks of wonder-filled worship to the Lord throughout this land, this timeline, this generation and for the generations to come. It is a sound that our nation and the nations need. Without your sound, the message revealing the heart and mind of God is incomplete for Australia and other nations in the world that we live in. God is both male and female, your representation of God is necessary to fulfill the promises of God in this era.

When God, said "Let us make mankind in our image, in our likeness "he created them male and female (see Genesis 1: 26, 27). There is something that men and women separately carry, that reflects the image and likeness of God.
Your sound as women reflecting the image and likeness of God could be: your song, your dance, your music, your art, your preaching, teaching, impartation, activation, your intercession or your act of sharing of a word from the Lord with a friend. It could be sharing your God given gift, your smile, your love, or your hospitality. All of these things carry the sound of heaven and it's grounded in the word of God and the love of God. When it is intentionally released, all of heaven will partner with it, to see it accomplish all that the Lord intends it to accomplish.

I believe the Lord is just waiting to see who will say, 'yes Lord, send me' (see Isaiah 6:8). 'Yes Lord I will be your handmaiden' (see Luke 1:38 in the AMPC). 'I will lay down my own thoughts, opinions, ideas and I will run into your wrap around presence and dwell in the tent of meeting.' 'I will abide in your presence.' 'I will surrender my all to you, to know you and sup with you.' 'I will lay down my life for you, to see your tender loving goodness transform and reform my people, our families, our communities, our city, town, and our nation.'

I love Mary's response when the angel of the Lord announced to her that she will give birth to the Son of God. This is her response:

> *38 Then Mary said, Behold, I am the handmaiden of the Lord; let it be done to me according to what you have said. And the angel left her.* (Luke 1:38 AMPC)

'Let it be done to me!!' Oh my goodness. I cannot imagine the level of yielding that was required by Mary, in this context, in these times. She was a young single girl, engaged not married, a virgin yet pregnant.

The Passion Translation (TPT) footnotes from Luke 1:26-27 tells us that 'Mary was betrothed to Joseph. This betrothal period usually lasted one year, and unfaithfulness on the part of the bride during the engagement would have been punishable by death.'

Joseph, the one she is betrothed to at the time doesn't know what to think. Joseph must have grappled with many scenarios wondering how this could be. What was he to think? He didn't want to publicly disgrace Mary. Matthew 1:19 tells us that he 'planned to divorce her quietly.' That is, until the angel of the Lord visited him. Joseph must have wondered what family and relatives would have thought.　Nothing in all of history past had ever happened before like this, and yet Mary remained steadfast in her trust, surrender and devotion to the Lord.

I am so inspired by the joy Mary exuded as she sang a prophetic song in verses 46-55. The Passion Translation (TPT) version is thrilling. Let me just give you the first four verses.

> [46] And Mary sang this song: "My soul is ecstatic, overflowing with praises to God! [47] My spirit bursts with joy over my life-giving God! [48] For he set his tender gaze upon me, his lowly servant girl. And from here on, everyone will know that I have been favoured and blessed. [49] The Mighty One has worked a mighty miracle for me; holy is his name! (TPT)

There is an invitation to surrender all to the Lord, no matter your natural or cultural situation, to go deep into the sacred, secret place with Him (see Isaiah 45:3), with the fear of the Lord (see Isaiah 11:3) and with a heart cry of holy, holy, holy is the Lord God Almighty (see Revelations 4:8). Right now, everything in me is screaming Oh Lord, send me.

For some of you (Tiddas) it has felt like it's been a long time coming. I want to encourage you, the time has now come! I sense that all of heaven is announcing 'who is this that bursts forth like the dawning of a new day.'

> *"Who is this, arising like the dawn, as fair as the moon, as bright as the sun, as majestic as an army with billowing banners"* (Song of Songs 6:10 NLT)

> *"Who is this woman? She is like the sunrise in all of its glory. She is as beautiful as the moon. She is as bright as the sun. She is as majestic as the stars travelling across the sky"* (Song of Songs 6:10 NIRV)

Tidda, that's you, the Beloved's Bride! This is you, beautiful, courageous daughter of the King. Wow! How beautiful you are!

The change of posture, position and the coming out!

This is the time to come out from hiding. Some of you might consider that you have been tucked away where no one can touch you but …

I feel the Lord say:

'I am breaking you out from behind the rock, and breaking you forth to stand on the rock. I am unveiling the raw beauty of my bride. I am raising you up to display my splendour'

For a long time, some of you have felt like you have been hidden under a rock but

I hear the Lord say:

'I have hidden you in the cleft of the rock and now is the time to Come forth – arise!'

Tiddas I call you forth into your destiny this day. I speak over you 'arise and come out from under the rock, step out of hiding and into your destiny.' 'In Jesus name.'

Many have been earthbound in the natural, and not able to rise. Now Jesus, the lover of your soul will cause you to *arise* with the *'tide of the times',* in this new era. This is your season, your *time to arise and shine.* Yes *arise and shine for your light has come and the glory of the Lord has risen upon you* (Isaiah 60:1).

As I was reading and meditating on Isaiah 60, I had a revelation that I want to share with you. In a vision, I saw the silhouette of a human. I knew it represented all people. This silhouette was filled with, and spilled out with a luminous and glorious light. The light beamed with brilliance from every angle. The light beaming from inside of this silhouette was majestic.

The revelation I had was that this light is Jesus himself, who rises within us, and shines through us. I could say it like this: *'arise and shine for the light of Christ has come up from within you. The glory of the Lord himself rises up and shines out of you.'* Jesus, the light of the world rises upon you and shines through you into all the world. Your light is so bright, people around you will need to wear their sunglasses.
So next time you feel dull, dim and unseen, simply re-adjust your thinking, renew your mind, because Tidda, you shine the light of Christ. You are one with Him (see 1 Corinthians 6:17). 'Ain't no one gonna' breeze past Christ in you without noticing how brightly you shine!

I decree over you the words the Lord said to me:

No longer shall you hide your light under a bushel. This time again, I say 'let there be light'!! The Genesis light will stream forth bringing new life and freshness. My light will be released afresh through the sound of the Tiddas, whose mouths I am filling, whose eyes I am opening, whose ears will hear my voice with crystal clear clarity.

The Lord is releasing His light through you in many different ways.

People don't hide a lamp under a bowl. They put it on a lampstand. Then the light shines for everyone in the house. (Matthew 5:15 ERV)

Neither do men light a candle and put it under a bushel but on a candlestick; and it giveth light unto all that are in the house. (Matthew 5:15 KJV)

And people don't light a lamp and then hide it under a ·bowl [or basket].
They put it on a lampstand so the light shines for all the people in the house. (Matthew 5:15 EXB)

2 Now the earth was formless and empty, darkness was over the surface of the deep, and the Spirit of God was hovering over the waters. 3 And God said, "Let there be light," and there was light. 4 God saw that the light was good, and he separated the light from the darkness. (Genesis 1:2-4 NIV)

The power of the 'Genesis' light, through God speaking it into being, was powerful to light up the world and would do so every single day at sunrise. The power of God speaking to us today through His word in the Bible, prophetic words, decrees and proclamations, still carries the same power to create and re-create, to resurrect dreams, visions, and prophetic words over your life.

Get ready, the Lord is calling you 'to come out from' the place of just accepting the status quo, 'to rise up out of' unbelief, 'to step out of' the place of lack. 'To step into' the *Philippians 4:13* place that says 'I'm ready', I can do all things through Christ who strengthens me.

> *12 I know what it is to be in need, and I know what it is to have plenty. I have learned the secret of being content in any and every situation, whether well fed or hungry, whether living in plenty or in want. 13 I can do all this through him who gives me strength. 14 Yet it was good of you to share in my troubles.* (Philippians 4:12-14 NIV)

> *12–13 I know what it means to lack, and I know what it means to experience overwhelming abundance. For I'm trained in the secret of overcoming all things, whether in fullness or in hunger. And I find that the strength of Christ's explosive power infuses me to conquer every difficulty. 14 You've so graciously provided for my essential needs during this season of difficulty.* (Philippians 4:12-14 TPT)

Even now as I write this, for me personally as a Tidda, it is part of the breaking out; breaking through and breaking into:

'*Breaking out*' of the past position of shrinking back, hiding and not being heard;

'*Breaking through*' to a place of embracing a more empowered and higher way, seated with Christ, at the right hand of the Father, to co-rule and reign with Christ, and take dominion over the enemy and;

'*Breaking into*' a greater place of living from a position of '*in Him I live and move and have my being*', and a place of '*He is the same yesterday today and tomorrow*'. This is a place of truly living in greater maturity in your new identity as the daughter of God arising to advance the Kingdom of God in our communities and throughout the nations of the earth.

As I write this, and as a Tidda myself, I feel a new level of freedom, and a *Joshua 1:6,7,9 and 18* boldness and courage to express what I believe the Lord is saying in these times. So Tidda, be very strong and courageous.

I believe in this new era, we will see many of the Tiddas from Australia and many other countries *breaking out* of a contained place; *breaking through* to be positioned to lead and govern, and *breaking into* a position of true Kingdom identity, maturity and purpose. I see them living firmly rooted in the love of God, wielding the sword of the Spirit to govern in this new era.

As an Australian First Nations Tidda, I believe this applies to First Nation Australian women, but I also believe this call to arise and shine in boldness and courage is a call to all First Nation women around the world.

The Turn-Around Anointing

I heard the Lord speak again:

'The enemy has robbed the Tiddas for too long, but now I am turning the tide.'

There are two points in a turning tide. One is at LOW tide, and the second is at HIGH tide.

I hear the Lord, this second say:

'It is High Tide and High Time for The Tide of Turnaround to turn what was meant for evil around for good.'

There is a 'turnaround anointing' being released on the TIDDAS in this new era. The tide has turned and I am restoring all that the cankerworm has stolen. Dreams, desires and visions, glorious riches, and more than you could ever hope for, dream of or imagine will be 'restored and poured' out on you, in you and through you.

In the Spirit I am hearing the words:

"RESTORATION, RESTITUTION AND RECOMPENSE"

This is what the Lord is doing in this era.

DEFINITION OF RESTITUTION:

Restitution is the restoration of something lost or stolen to its proper owner.

I will restore what the locust and the cankerworm has stolen!

> *"I shall restore to you the years that the locust, the swarming locust, the canker-worm and the caterpillar have eaten ....."* (Joel 2:25 TLV)

In Joel 2, we read about a situation facing Judah where there hadn't been rain for years, the pastures in the wilderness had dried up and the wild animals were starving. The fig tree and vines had no fruit, and whatever green shoots there were, were consumed by hordes of swarming locusts. In the midst of this bleak situation God promises a turn around that would change everything.

God promised "I will repay you for the years the locusts have eaten, and I will send the autumn and spring rains. Your threshing floors will be full of grain and your vats will overflow with new wine and oil". (Joel 2:23-25). God brought a great restoration of their fortunes

DEFINITION OF RECOMPENSE:

Recompense means to make amends to someone for loss or harm suffered, compensate.

> *Instead of your (former) shame you shall have a twofold recompense; instead of dishonour and reproach (your people) shall rejoice in their portion. Therefore in their land they shall possess double (what they had forfeited); everlasting joy shall be theirs.* (Isaiah 61:7 AMPC)

Get ready to usher in the tide of turnaround. As the Tiddas respond to the call and step into their destiny, the act of stepping in, pierces the invisible force field that has been separating them from their inheritance in heaven.

Tidda, as you step in, you activate the *double portion*. The double portion of rejoicing and joy that will be released, the glorious riches of heaven that are yet to be revealed (and not like you might imagine) will manifest in glorious ways.

Tiddas, "this double portion, that is breaking forth will swiftly turn you from the distractions that would lure you away from My presence". It will turn you and deliver you from the snares of the enemy. The double portion turnaround will set the course for your victory run.

There is a double portion promise for the TIDDAS ARISING. I am sensing a great celebration on this,

I hear in the Spirit many voices exclaiming:

'What a turnout, what a turnout!'

They are all here to witness the Tiddas arise.

We are seeing beauty for ashes, the oil of joy instead of mourning, a garment of praise instead of a spirit of despair. They will be called oaks of righteousness, a planting of the Lord for the display of His splendour.

> *.... and provide for those who grieve in Zion— to bestow on them a crown of beauty instead of ashes, the oil of joy instead of mourning, and a garment of praise instead of a spirit of despair. They will be called oaks of righteousness, a planting of the Lord for the display of his splendour* (Isaiah 61:3 NIV).

> *... to strengthen those crushed by despair who mourn in Zion— to give them a beautiful bouquet in the place of ashes, the oil of bliss instead of tears, and the mantle of joyous praise instead of the spirit of heaviness. Because of this, they will be known as Mighty Oaks of Righteousness, planted by Yahweh as a living display of his glory.* (Isaiah 61:3 TPT)

We are seeing an exchange taking place. Tiddas are trading-in years of tears, grief and despair for the sound of joy and praise that is filling their temple and filling the atmosphere.

Midwives, Be On Your Guard. Guard the Birthing!

As the waves break, the waters break, and a birthing breaks forth.

The Lord spoke:

The birthing of my shining ones, who send forth rays in the likeness of my Son, the glorious one.

Tiddas are being *birthed in this hour* to *shine in these times*. Midwives gather round. Come around those Tiddas being birthed in this hour. I sense an urgency for the midwives to gather around them, to protect the right of passage as they pass through the birthing canal to receive their heavenly birthright.

The midwives are the Non-Indigenous and the First Nations women, and women of all nationalities, the maternal, mature ones.

The atmosphere was charged with warning:

.... *"And the dragon crouched before the woman who was about to give birth – poised to devour the baby the moment it was born"*. (Revelation 12:4 TPT)

Midwives on guard, gather round and *guard the birthing*. Your warrior wisdom and experience speaks life as you lead and guide the birth of the next generation of 'Tiddas Arising.'

As you guard the birthing, do it from a place of joined hearts, with all your heart, all your mind and all your strength, as unto the Father. Do it in the Spirit of covenant oneness with Father and oneness with each other. It is the guard formed by the unity and one-ness of heart that will guard the sacred birthings in the lands in this hour. I sense God saying, *'job well done'*.

Tiddas Beware of the Enemy's Snare

As the wave breaks, the waters break, you are birthed, and you *hit the ground running.* I hear the words:

'Beware the enemy's snare'

The Lord in His kindness alerts us and implores us:

> "*Therefore, since we are surrounded by such a great cloud of witnesses, let us throw off everything that hinders, and the sin that so easily entangles. And let us run with perseverance the race marked out for us*" (Hebrews 12:1 NIV). Other versions say '*the race set before us*'

Right here, could I encourage us to throw off the snares of temptation, shame and torment. Throw off comparison, competition and self-bitterness. Throw off un-forgiveness, bitterness, doubt and unbelief. Throw off the very thing that could so easily entangle us.

Jesus came to *set the captives free* (see Isaiah 61:3) and *reset the mindsets of old.* Do not be conformed but be transformed by the renewing of your mind (see Romans 12:2). You cannot stand, let alone run forward ensnared with such hindrances. Don't let the dragon steal what is being birthed. Tiddas - on guard, Midwives - on guard.

Tiddas, throw off shame, condemnation, comparison and competition. Declare *truth and truce.* Determine to *run together* in *covenant relationship and oneness.*

There is an *acceleration* on this as you *hit the ground running*. Tidda "*run straight for the invitation of reaching the heavenly goal and gaining the victory – prize through the anointing of Jesus*" (Philippians 3:14 TPT)

The New Sound

The arising of the *Tiddas* gives *voice* to an ancient cry that resounds across the land. The land cries out. The earth groans and travails for the revealing of the sons and daughters of God. Here come the daughters of destiny.

> *For [even the whole] creation (all nature) waits expectantly and longs earnestly for God's sons to be made known [waits for the revealing, the disclosing of their sonship].* (Romans 8:19 AMPC)

> *The entire universe is standing on tiptoe, yearning to see the unveiling of God's glorious sons and daughters!* (Romans 8:19 TPT)

There is a *new sound* coming forth from the waves and from the lands as the Tiddas arise. It is the sound of First Nations Sisters breaking forth, to be sent forth into the nation, and throughout the nations. This voice, a vital chord that has been missing in the vocal scale of heaven's symphony. I believe this is part of the earth groaning and travailing, like a woman in childbirth waiting for the sons and daughters to arise.

> [22] *We know that the whole creation has been groaning in travail together until now;* (Romans 8:22 RSV)

> *We know that everything God made has been waiting until now in pain like a woman ready to give birth to a child.* (Romans 8:22 ERV)

A new sound, of the *tide of Tiddas'* is rising.

There are sounds of weeping, groaning, laughing, joy, shouts of victory and celebrations. Sounds of many joining the army. Sounds of the remnant army rising; the sound of locking shields, and the sound of wonder-filled worship to the Lord. A glorious sound of heaven and earth merging. The sound of all of us, merging as one with Father and one with another. The sound of angel armies taking flight, and taking their place at the side of the Tiddas. The sound of the generations joining as one. The sound of our Non-Indigenous brothers and sisters, communities and families joining forces with us. The sound of one warrior Bride rising as one.

The great cloud of witnesses cheering you on as you *arise, shine* and *run* for Jesus!

I believe the nations need the Tiddas, with all their unique mantles, giftings, graces and mandates. The Tiddas are a vital part of the bigger picture and the greater plan to see revival, reformation and transformation in our nation and the nations. I believe this is one of the ancient keys to the new sound rising from the land.

Just as a body without a nose or eyes is incomplete, so too the Body of Christ is incomplete until every part of the body take their place and work together as a unified force.

This end time move of God involves much, including the following three aspects. The first is a revival that will see an unprecedented harvest of souls. The second is a reformation of the church to restore it to its original design, power and impact. Finally a reformed church will bring transformation of every aspect of society as the Kingdom of God emerges in power.

For the church to emerge in the earth as a transforming instrument of change, the body needs to be complete with every part taking their place. The Body is incomplete without the First Nations people, and Tiddas rising up empowered and equipped to do what only they have been ordained to do to advance the Kingdom of God in the earth. Tiddas, you have been designed to do what no other can do in these times. Tidda, for such a time as this!

How can we usher this in together?

First and foremost, let us seek and ask Holy Spirit how we can usher in this new thing.

This is an invitation for every believer to join forces and partner with what God is doing in this era. This invitation is for all leaders and each person in the body of Christ, men and women, First Nations and Non-Indigenous to usher this in together. Let us join forces to take our nations for Jesus. Let us all cheer one another on. Let us make way for and come alongside the Tiddas and one another to all rise together. May the Fathers and Mothers nurture the Tiddas who respond to this call to arise. It will be exciting to mentor and journey with the Tiddas arising, to call forth the Tiddas and walk with them, young and old, as they are called to come out from under the rock to arise and shine in this season.

This invitation is for you to partner with this heavenly call to connect, to come around, to guard and guide, to cheer on and to champion the Tiddas arising in your sphere!

Tidda, this is your invitation to be strong and fearless as you step out of your comfort zone, out of the familiar place, and step into the destiny to which you are called. *Daughter of destiny*, steward well the voice that the Lord is giving you. Arise and lead!

Let us expect to see First Nations women, in all Nations, beginning to rise within the seven mountains and across the five-fold ministry, with increased spheres of influence. Let us facilitate heavenly partnerships that no man can tear down. Let us decree that men and women from every tribe, tongue and nation are running together to see the Kingdom of God established across this great Nation of Australia and the throughout the nations. Let us, together, be the Kingdom army rising up, taking the land, exalting the Almighty God.

TIDDAS - ARISE, SHINE AND RUN FOR JESUS!

I love you!
Katie x

Footnotes:

1. Healing Wounded Hearts – Holy Spirit directed Inner Healing authored by Katherine and Peter Dunstan Available @ amazon.com.au

2. Divine Union
   Author: Peter Dunstan Available @ amazon.com.au

Chapter 3

Grafted - In

16 Now if the first handful of dough offered as the first-fruits [Abraham and the patriarchs] is consecrated (holy), so is the whole mass [the nation of Israel]; and if the root [Abraham] is consecrated (holy), so are the branches.

17 But if some of the branches were broken off, while you, a wild olive shoot, were grafted in among them to share the richness [of the root and sap] of the olive tree,

18 Do not boast over the branches and pride yourself at their expense. If you do boast and feel superior, remember it is not you that support the root, but the root [that supports] you.

(Romans 11:16-18 AMPC)

The Holy Land and the Land Down Under

(Encounters in Outback Australia and Israel)

I would like to share encounters I had that revealed to me the same message in two geographical locations, Israel and outback Australia. There are four encounters, two revealed a message of being *grafted-in*, and the other two encounters revealed a message of *inter-generational connection, blessing and alignment*. In this chapter we will journey together through four encounters, two Countries, two messages.

The message of being *'grafted-in'* came to me once in the Holy Land of Israel and again in the land down under, outback Australia.

The message of *'inter-generational connection and alignment'* also came to me while I was in Israel and a second time in outback Australia.

Australia is one of the farthest lands geographically from Israel. In the Great Commission, Jesus sent his disciples to Jerusalem, all Judea and Samaria, and to the ends of the earth. From Jerusalem, Australia, New Zealand and the Pacific Islands, all of which are a part of The Great Southlands of the Holy Spirit, represent the ends of the earth.

The encounters also carry an inter-generational element to them. They span in time, from ancient times before the foundation of the earth to the current era. The messages revealed from the encounters, I believe, contain ancient keys to unlock the new era.

But you will receive power when the Holy Spirit comes on you; and you will be my witnesses in Jerusalem, and in all Judea and Samaria, and to the ends of the earth." (Acts 1:8 NIV)

Grafted-In:

In 2019 we travelled throughout Outback Australia. We crossed four States (New South Wales, Queensland, Western Australia and Northern Territory), covering over 10,000 kilometres. It was in the middle of summer with temperatures rising up to 45 degrees Celsius. The air-conditioning in our car stopped working right when the temperature peaked. What an adventure we were on and we were so grateful for the opportunity! How grateful we were to eventually get the air-conditioning fixed to resume travel with cool air again. We towed our caravan (home on wheels) through the Kimberley Country in Western Australia, Northern Territory and Far North Queensland. We were incredibly privileged to travel this part of our journey with an Apostolic Father and Mother to this nation of Australia, Pastors Tim and Di Edwards (1). Actually, we were with them while in Israel also. Thank you Jesus for the gift they are to us, to our nation and the nations. We love them dearly. Apostle Tim and Di, we honour you both.

God's stunning creation and handiwork in our land down under is nothing short of magnificent! Wow, Lord you are good. Thank you Lord for our incredibly gifted and amazing First Nations and Non-Indigenous warriors, who are championing and leading our outback First Nations people. Together, they are labouring in love to advance the Kingdom of God so powerfully, in the presence, power and wisdom of the Lord God Almighty.

To these current day heroes in the faith, we love you, we honour you, we champion you, and set our hearts in agreement with you - to see the Kingdom come and God's will be done in the lives of our families, communities, tribes and people, in Jesus name. The Spirit of God is moving powerfully across our nation. Amen!

First, I would like to share with you a diary entry from one of the days during this precious time in the outback. It reads like this:

Today I am seeing in the Spirit and I sense something *'grand of His Kingdom plan'*. This part of the word is for *all 'First Generation Christians'* of all nationalities, and especially for *'First Nation - First Generation Christians'*. I believe it is an important key for every person and nationality in this era.

Any person of any nationality that is the first one in their family generation to become a Christians, this word is for you. Also if you are of First Nations heritage and you were the first one in your family to become a Christian, this is for you. If you are one person in your family and you have other cousin brother or sisters who are Christians and they are in your generation, this word is for you. So no Uncles, Aunties, Mum or Dad or anyone else in the older generation were Christians – you are a *First Nations First-Generation Christian* and this word is for you. Each one of you reading this who is not a *first generation Christian*, I recommend that you keep reading, this chapter reveals more about the 'Ancient Keys to unlock the New Era'. That said, this chapter is an important link for you, for myself and for people of every tongue, tribe and nation to arise together in preparation for the greatest awakening coming to the nations.

Vision: Grafted In

In the land of Australia, while going out into Central Australia, the Lord took me into a vision where I could see needle-work happening in the spirit, just like a tapestry. The strong sense surrounding this needlework was that it was weaving thread into something grand. The hand of the Lord was weaving the thread in and through the base of the grand tapestry.

The needlework was neat and precise. The thread itself was a deep red colour, it was doubled and then doubled again, and doubled again. Three times it was doubled, creating a triple strength thread. It represented a strong foundation that would not be pulled apart, just as a three strand cord is not easily broken.

My sense is that the Lord is weaving us (*First Generation Christians* and *First Nations – First Generation* Christians) into a deep, rich, far reaching well spring of life that stems from a multi-generational Christian heritage. We are being grafted-in to the heritage of Christians who come from a long line of Christian Mothers, Fathers, and Grandparents. Even for some, the line of Christianity goes back four and more generations, to Grandparents' Grandparents and their Grandparents. This is the generational heritage that the Lord is weaving us into, all *First Generation Christians*.

Right now as I write this, I am so touched by the heart of Father God that He would do this for me, for you, and for so many others. His mercy, His kindness, His compassion, is tangible, I am flooded with His everlasting love and I am wrecked writing this.

As we travelled this ancient land, I was aware of the richly stunning red dirt in this part of Australia. However, in comparison, the red colour of the thread being used in this needlework, was way more captivating and breath-taking than the creation of the landscape surrounding us. For this thread represented the Creator himself and the blood of Jesus. Nothing compares. The triple thickness of the thread represents the strength and power of the blood of Jesus, linked to the three cord strand that is not easily broken. That three cord strand, is of course, the trinity: Father, Son and Holy Spirit. The thrice doubled thread represents the unshakeable foundation of Christ, the rock of all ages, timelines, dimensions and generations.

I want to encourage you, if you are a *first generation Christian* in your family line and seemingly have no Christian heritage, do not be discouraged, but rather be encouraged. The Lord is about the Father's business, He is grafting you into a rich tapestry of eternal heritage called *Kingdom Family* that spans the ages and positions you to take hold of your generational Kingdom inheritance.

Timeline of Restoration and Multiplication

He is bringing us in, we are entering into a timeline of *'restoration and multiplication.'* He is *'restoring His original intent'* for our whole lives, not just from when we became a Christian. The Lord is moving through the timeline of your life, right back to the time of conception and He is taking back what the enemy stole from our lives in Christ. He is restoring the original plan and purpose He has for your life.

For I know the plans I have for you, declares the Lord, plans to prosper you and not to harm you, but to give you hope and a future (Jeremiah 29:11 NIV)

He is showing himself strong to increase and multiply the rich generational blessings.

He is grafting His beloved ones into the *'family tree'* to share in the rich generational blessings, the strong spiritual life, and the ancient wisdom of generations gone before us.

Grafting you in Romans 11:17

*But if some of the branches were broken off, while you, a wild olive shoot, were **grafted in** among them to share the richness [of the root and sap] of the olive tree, (AMPC)*

*[17] However, some of the branches have been pruned away. And you, who were once nothing more than a wild olive branch in the desert, **God has grafted in**— inserting you among the remaining branches **as a joint partner** to share in the wonderful richness of the cultivated olive stem. [18] So don't be so arrogant as to believe that you are superior to the natural branches. There's no reason to boast, for the new branches don't support the root, but you owe your life to the root that supports you! (TPT)*

The root is Jesus! You owe your life to Jesus who supports you. I owe my life to Jesus who supports me.

In Romans 11 Paul explains how God has grafted the gentile believers into the tree which is Israel. Jesus uses a similar analogy of a vine, to illustrate that we are part of the vine which is Christ, and the life of Christ flows into us as we abide in Him.

His life flowing through us is so critical that Jesus says, "apart from me you can do nothing." So, not only are we grafted into Israel, we are grafted into the vine which is Christ himself.

Jesus said, *"I am the true vine, and my Father is the gardener. He cuts off every branch in me that bears no fruit, while every branch that does bear fruit he prunes so that it will be even more fruitful. You are already clean because of the word I have spoken to you. Remain in me, as I also remain in you. No branch can bear fruit by itself; it must remain in the vine. Neither can you bear fruit unless you remain in me. "I am the vine; you are the branches. If you remain in me and I in you, you will bear much fruit; apart from me you can do nothing.* (John 15:1-5 NIV)

The enemy has tried to rob us of our God given heritage and Kingdom inheritance, but the Lord is releasing a fresh revelation of being *'grafted in,* in great power that will empower *all first generation Christians* of every nationality, and especially His *First Nations- first generation* believers.

There is a shift taking place in greater magnitude, from a position of *'orphan to extended family,'* from *'Sonship to Fathering and Mothering.'* From a position of struggling to take your place to being positioned to lead the nation. This is not only for First generation believers, this is for second, third, fourth generation believers and beyond.

You are grafted-in as co-heirs with Christ to rule and reign with an ancient mandate to govern the earth. I believe as we go and multiply, we are to reproduce sons and daughters who grow and mature to take their place as Mothers and Fathers in the Kingdom family, to raise up the family generations to come.

God wants you to know that He is grafting you into something that spans the timelines of heaven and there are generational blessings for you.

Encounter with Jesus in Israel at the Garden of Gethsemane

The second encounter I am about to share with you happened when I was physically in the Holy Land of Israel in 2018. We were a part of two different delegations. We were a part of an Indigenous Trade Mission. This was a delegation of Australian Indigenous business and community leaders invited by the Director General of Ministry of Foreign Affairs of Israel for the purpose of trade and cultural exchange. This was an important connection between two First Nation peoples to open doors of trade and culture.

One highlight of the Trade Mission was being part of a meeting at the Knesset in the President's official residence, where the delegation presented a precious scroll that had been crafted from kangaroo skin. This scroll had been signed by many First Nation Christian Elders and community leaders to decree that the Christian First Nation people of Australia stand with Israel. What an awesome privilege, honour and blessing to be part of this covenant making moment joining hearts, cultures and countries in the Spirit realm in God's timeline. I honour all who were involved.

The other amazing reason we were in Israel was to join the 2018 Israel Tour with Dr Brian and Candice Simmons, Wesley and Stacey Campbell, Mark and Ann Tubbs and other wonderful leaders.

I was in the Garden of Gethsemane. It was here in this geographical location in the Holy Land where I was taken into a life altering spiritual encounter.

Jesus' love for First Nation peoples

From the moment the encounter began, I physically felt the presence and power of God come, up through the land and it began to rise up, through my feet, and into the rest of my body until I was completely consumed by the Spirit of God. By this time I was deep weeping from the depths of my being. My Spirit man was awakened to a larger realm. It was as if I had just stepped into a spiritual well of glory oil. The anointing was powerful.

In that consumed state in the encounter, in the Spirit God took me down a 2000+year old generational timeline, all the way to Jesus in the garden of Gethsemane. It seemed a long way but yet a quick journey at high speed. Jesus was kneeling and as I was looking at Him, I felt Him with every fiber of my being. Here was Jesus, on His knees fully aware that He was about to give his life for the sins of the world. Yet, He turned to see me in that moment. Jesus stops to see you. This indescribable sensation of euphoric love/worship completely and utterly engulfed my whole being. I was mesmerised in a moment where a complete merger took place, a divine union in its entirety.

In that moment, Jesus released just a glimpse of an *intense and ancient love* Jesus has for our First Nations people. I felt this all-consuming, overwhelming, and powerful transformational love. I just don't have any words that can begin to describe this love of God. I knew it was for First Nations people in Australia and First Nations people in every Country in the world.

I was struck with the reality that Jesus was about to give His life for us as First Nations people. Now, we know that Jesus died on the cross for all humanity, but in this encounter it was made real to me that Jesus was about to hang on the cross for our people, First Nations people groups.

> *For God so loved the world that He gave His only begotten Son, that whoever believes in Him should not perish but have everlasting life.* (John 3:16 NKJV)

> *For God so greatly loved and dearly prized the world that He [even] gave up His only begotten (unique) Son, so that whoever believes in (trusts in, clings to, relies on) Him shall not perish (come to destruction, be lost) but have eternal (everlasting) life.* (John 3:16 AMPC)

Other versions say 'gave His only begotten Son, gave His one and only Son; gave his only and unique Son; gave *His* only-born Son; special son,; and Dr Brian Simmons in The Passion Translation says 'gave his only, unique Son *as a gift.'*

God gave (sacrificed) His son Jesus as a gift and Jesus willingly gave His own life for you, for me, for our First Nations people all over the world, for all humanity.

I was so completely undone and have never been the same since that moment in time, in Israel, in the Garden of Gethsemane with Jesus!

That love of God, is a deep love that plumbs the depth of time, and spans the timelines, ages and dimensions. The height of His love draws you into heights of heavenly encounters. It is a love that reaches from the foundations of the earth, back in time and to eternity. It extends much farther than your eye can see, your mind can imagine, your heart can fathom and wider than the reach of the outstretched arms of Jesus on the cross that reaches to the heavens and spans the whole earth. It reaches to every human heart and life on the planet, past, present and future, and on to eternity. I just don't have the words to describe this love of God, a God who is love.

An ancient key to unlock the new era is to grasp and embrace how wide and high, long and deep is the love of God for the First Nations people in Australia and around the world. May we be able to receive and withstand the glory of the tiny glimpse of the love God has for us.

> [17] *so that Christ may dwell in your hearts through faith. And I pray that you, being rooted and established in love,* [18] *may have power, together with all the Lord's holy people, to grasp how wide and long and high and deep is the love of Christ,* [19] *and to know this love that surpasses knowledge—that you may be filled to the measure of all the fullness of God.* (Ephesians 3:17-19 NIV)

> [17] *Then, by constantly using your faith, the life of Christ will be released deep inside you, and the resting place of his love will become the very source and root of your life.* [18-19] *Then you will be empowered to discover what every holy one experiences—the great magnitude of the astonishing love of Christ in all its dimensions. How deeply intimate and far-reaching is his love! How enduring and inclusive it is!*

Endless love beyond measurement that transcends our understanding—this extravagant love pours into you until you are filled to overflowing with the fullness of God! (Ephesians 3:17-19 TPT)

After the encounter in the Garden, I was still weeping from somewhere deeper inside of my limited being, when Stacey Campbell came up to me, she placed her hand on my shoulder, looked at me and said 'the connection, it's an Indigenous thing'. She recognised First Nations connectedness to the land. Oh my gosh! It released the floodgates of a *deep, generational inner-healing* within me. I knew I was to take this back to my homeland and testify about Jesus' love for our people groups.

The Bible says 'The testimony of Jesus is the spirit of prophecy' (see Revelation 10:19) and as we speak about what Jesus has done, it has the power to say 'do it again Lord.' I believe that as I share this testimony of Jesus, and as you read this and place yourself in this testimony, the power and Spirit of prophecy will be released to do to our people, what Jesus did for me as Stacey spoke over me. I believe it has the life on it to bring a *deep, generational inner-healing* to you, our First Nations people, as you place yourself in this story of deep love and sheer purity, and receive revelation of the fierce transforming love of God for you.

The Garden of Gethsemane was such a significant location in the whole journey, from the last supper to the crucifixion. Isaiah 53 speaks of the sufferings of Christ. In verse 5 we read:

"He was pierced for our transgressions, he was crushed for our iniquities". (Isaiah 53:5 TPT)

Jesus was pierced at Calvary, but was crushed at Gethsemane.

Dr Brian Simmons the author of The Passion Translation shares in his notes: the word "Gethsemane" means "oil press", and it was located on the lower slopes of the Mount of Olives. It was here in Gethsemane where the olives were pressed into oil. It was here that the sins of all mankind were placed on Jesus' sacred shoulders and he would experience an overwhelming crushing of his soul.

It was at this very place that my husband and I stood, our footprint in Jesus's footprint. Matthew records that Jesus became sorrowful and troubled (26:38) and then said to the disciples, "My soul is overwhelmed with sorrow to the point of death.

Three times Jesus asked that the cup be taken from Him (Matt 26). What was in the cup that caused Jesus such grief and pain? I too believe the cup that Jesus drank from was the cup of the wrath of the Almighty (refer Job 21:20, Jeremiah 25:15, Isaiah 51:17, and Isaiah 51:22). The punishment, and the wrath of God that was to be our rightful judgement, Jesus drank in full. This was His crushing, this is what left him grief stricken and overwhelmed to the point of death.

In Hebrews we read, *"During Christ's days on earth he pleaded with God, praying with passion and with tearful agony that God would spare him from death. And because of his perfect devotion his prayer was answered and he was delivered"*. (Hebrews 5:7 TPT). Dr Simmons expresses this: I believe the moment that the writer to the Hebrews is referring to, is the time Jesus was in the Garden. I believe that Jesus prayer was that he wouldn't die in the Garden from the sheer overwhelm, and God "spared him from death" so that he could go on to Calvary to complete what he came to do. At Calvary He would be "lifted up" (John 12:32) and "pierced for our transgressions" (Isaiah 53:5)

It was in the soil of the Garden of Gethsemane that Jesus sweat fell like drops of blood (Luke 22:44). If the blood of Abel called out from the ground "justice" then the sweat and the blood of Jesus speak a better word, "forgiveness" (Hebrews 12:24 TPT)
The penalty for sin has been paid by Jesus in full.

> *"After this I looked, and there before me was a great multitude that no one could count, from every nation, tribe, people and language, standing before the throne and before the Lamb. They were wearing white robes and were holding palm branches in their hands.* (Revelation 7:9 NIV)

In that great multitude are First Nations People from every generation and every Indigenous nation.

Encounter in Israel: Unclaimed Blessings

This third encounter was in Israel. It was one of the many prophetic encounters I had with the Lord during our time in Israel. I felt led to share this one, along with the above in this book.
While travelling across the Holy Land and immersing myself in the life and walk of Jesus, the Lord took me into an encounter with Him, where we travelled down the timeline of generations. It was a generational timeline of Israel. As we went, Jesus would pause and point to the left, he said to me '*look daughter*', then we would travel some more, He stopped and pointed to the right. Again He said to me '*look, daughter*'. As we took this journey together the Lord was showing me '*unclaimed blessings*' as we passed through each year and through each generation. These blessings were just sitting '*in waiting*', waiting to be claimed.

I felt the Lord say to me 'these are the many *unclaimed blessings* throughout the generations, claim them and draw them into the "now generation", call them forth into your life and into the lives of this generation and the generations to come.

Each **"unclaimed generational blessing"** is a '**seed in waiting'**. Each seed carries the Spirit of **"eternal life"** that spans the generations gone and the generations to come.

Each seed of unclaimed blessing, is impregnated with resurrection life-giving power, to birth into the natural realm that which has been conceived in the supernatural realm.
I believe there is a supernatural aspect to these unclaimed blessings from the generations gone that the Lord wants to authorise, empower and assign to us in these times, as an ancient key to this new era.

There are seeds of unclaimed blessings that carry the eternal resurrection power to birth and bring forth into the natural realm the power of the supernatural realm.

Grafted-In

In Genesis 22 God said to Abraham, 'I will surely bless you, and make your descendants as numerous as the stars in the sky and the sand on the seashore. Your descendants will take possession of the cities of their enemies, and through their offspring all the nations of the earth will be blessed' (see vs 17, 18).

We as gentile believers are "grafted in" to Israel and are part of Israel. The blessings promised to the descendants of Abraham are our blessings (see Romans 11:17-18).

I believe we have authority to take hold of the unclaimed generational blessings and draw them into the now to prosper us and advance the Kingdom on earth, as it is in heaven.

So I encourage you to claim the blessings of Israel, Abraham and Jesus for your life. You are 'grafted in' to Israel. Israel's blessings are your blessings. You are grafted into Abraham (see Galatians 3:26-29), Abraham's blessing are your blessings.
You are also grafted into Jesus (see John 15:1-4), Jesus blessings are your blessings. Claim these blessings for your life, the 'unclaimed generational blessings sit in waiting. Call them forth into the 'now generation'. Decree and declare the blessings of Israel, Abraham and Jesus over your life and over the generations to come. (Romans 11:16-18; John 15:1-4).

These were ancient old unclaimed blessings being released into this era.
In my heart and Spirit, a deep revelation of being grafted into Israel consumed me. I began to weep for Israel from deep within like it was my homeland. It manifested in fervent prayer for Israel. Join with me on a life journey and determine in your heart to pray for the peace of Jerusalem and pray for the protection and rise of Israel.

> *Pray for the peace of Jerusalem: "May those who love you be secure. [7] May there be peace within your walls and security within your citadels."*
> (Psalm 122:5-7 NIV)

> *Pray and seek for Jerusalem's peace, for all who love her will prosper! [7] O Jerusalem, May there be peace for those who dwell inside your walls and prosperity in your every palace.* (Psalm 122:5-7 TPT).

The Eternal Baton of Honour

During my time journeying through outback Australia, I had the fourth encounter I would like to share with you in this chapter. I could see in the Spirit realm a large baton. This baton had markings on it and markings carved into it.

I somehow knew that these markings held the story and the journey of our old people who cried out in prayer for us; who have travailed for us; who declared the word of God over us; who sang worship songs over us; believed for us; and fought the good fight of faith for us.

This baton is a baton of Honour, an 'eternal baton of honour'.

The 'eternal baton' is being handed to us in the here and now, from the heroes of faith that have gone before us.

This eternal baton is a 'live baton' held by the modern day heroes of today who are alive and with us here on earth.

It is held by the Gatekeepers of our communities - our Christian Elders, our Apostles, Prophets, Teachers, Evangelists and Pastors, and held by our intercessors. This baton holds the ancient promises of heaven, the living word of God carved into it through the prayers of those who have gone before us.

> [39] *These, though commended by God for their great faith, did not receive what was promised* [40] *That promise has awaited us, who receive the better thing that God has provided in these last days, so that with us, our forebears might finally see the promise completed.*
> (Hebrews 11:39-40 The Voice)

> *39-40* *Not one of these people, even though their lives of faith were exemplary, got their hands on what was promised. God had a better plan for us: that their faith and our faith would come together to make one completed whole, their lives of faith not complete apart from ours.*
> (Hebrews 11:39-40 The Message)

Stories, generational blessings, generational ancient wisdom and revelation are etched into the baton that has been passed to us. The same baton we will pass on to the next generation and the generations to come. As it passes from one generation to next, a live portal of profound, supernatural encounter is infused with increased power through the generations. With each generation added to it, it releases an ever increasing ancient well of wisdom and revelation.

Intergenerational

It became clear to me that this *'eternal baton of honour'* contained an intergenerational component.
I started to see that we are an integrated part, grafted-into a continuous and cohesive intergenerational company. Just like we are grafted into Israel and grafted into Jesus. It's like a live thread of interconnectedness, from generation to generation. I liken it to a three strand cord, the heroes of faith, us and the Lord. A three strand cord that is not easily broken.

This intergenerational connectedness enables us to access ancient wisdom, revelation and understanding that is beyond this lifetime. The access equips us to join the special forces of heaven, to join their lifetime of faith with our lives of faith.

Our faith, the faith of the ancient ones and the faith of the more recent heroes of faith; all joined with the holy host of angels to see the promises of God fulfilled in the earth, giving glory to God. This is an ancient key to the new era.

This *'eternal baton of honour'* has a supernatural function to *restore, renew, and secure* our Kingdom inheritance. It spans the generations. It spans down through the generations of the many heroes of the faith, down through our generation and reaches into the future generations.

It is like a river that continuously flows from generation to generation. A generational river of supernatural power is being released and activated as we take hold of this eternal baton of honour and run with it for Jesus. Run the race of faith. When I see a baton I think of a race and running on a track.

> But none of these things move me; nor do I count my life dear to myself, so that I may finish my race with joy, and the ministry which I received from the Lord Jesus, to testify to the gospel of the grace of God. (Acts 20:24 NKJV)

> **24-25** Do you remember how, on a racing-track, every competitor runs, but only one wins the prize? Well, you ought to run with your minds fixed on winning the prize! Every competitor in athletic events goes into serious training. Athletes will take tremendous pains—for a fading crown of leaves. But our contest is for an eternal crown that will never fade.
> (1 Corinthians 9:24-25 PHILLIPS)

I am in awe of God right now as I write this, I'm sitting here in awe and reverence of the sheer kindness, and the purity of the love of Jesus, the lover of my soul.   Imagine the ancient wisdom, divine revelation, the depth of faith, and fullness of restoration, unending pouring out of the oil of love and the oil of joy, the unshakeable life anchoring hope; and the divine life-union with the one who is love, Jesus!

Encounter with the Great Cloud of Witnesses

More recently, I was taken up into the heavenly realms. And there, standing right in front of me was the great cloud of witnesses. I could recognise that among them were some of our First Nation Christian ancestors, elders and some younger ones. There they stood upright, victorious in all their glory. Right here in the moment something even more supernatural happened. As I looked closer, the Lord showed me down the timeline of *their* lives and into the *faith journey* of their life while they were still alive on earth.

This was a generational timeline. As I looked into their faces, I could see these markings on their face. The markings started from their eyes and went downward to the end of their jaw lines, where the face meets the neck. The Lord was showing me markings of tears streaming down their faces from times of travailing for us.

The Lord showed me their posture of prayer. Even though they were standing, the Lord showed me a picture of them inside their upright body but postured - on their knees - revealing the times they were crying out in prayer, decreeing the word of God over us, and calling those things that are not, as though they are.

Here, I would like to take a moment to Honour our past Christian elders, intercessors, and gatekeepers who have warfared for generations. Also to our present day apostles and prophets, evangelists, teachers and pastors of today who have been on the frontline battle field; pushing back the powers of darkness; taking back the ground the enemy stole; for us today to be able to step into the destiny God has for us, as a people group, and as a nation. A deep gratitude and heart-filled thank you to each one of you!! Praise Jesus for your faithfulness and never giving up the fight, and for never quitting the race.

Dutch Sheets (3) in his February 2, 2021 'Give Him 15' broadcast, said 'The last two verses of Hebrews 11 give us the amazing answer; they did not receive the fulfillment of their promises because *God wouldn't allow them to be "complete" without us.* That is incredible! We, today, are a continuation of these individuals' callings and assignments. The Greek word translated "complete" also means, "to finish; to mature; to reach the intended goal." Think about the ramifications of this: without us, God can't *finish* what He began through those saints; what He started through them cannot *mature* or *reach its intended goal* until we grab the **baton and run our leg of the race**.'

He goes on to say 'The generations are far more interconnected than most of us realize. In God's mind, *accomplishing something through our descendants is the same as doing it through us.*'

Dutch Sheets confirms and reinforces my experience and encounter with the great cloud of witnesses as he says this 'they sowed, we reap the promise fulfilled in our generation.
This is generational faith... It's a relay race. The baton passed down to us, from those who have been promoted to heaven.'

I (Katie) want to highlight that there is a *generational relay race* taking place right now in Australia and across the nations. We have generals who have gone before us and generals living amongst us right now, running *with* us. I see this baton strategically moving between the generations as one celebrates and honours the other. Let us run together older and younger generations. The garrison of the generations! Amen! A Garrison is a battalion. Together we are the army of the Lord running the great race and fighting the good fight of faith, taking ground together.

There has been past generations that have sown through prayer, intercession, travailing, and sowed into this moment we are stepping into right now! We have the privilege of living in the fulfilment of the promise. Our ancestors who are up with the great cloud of witnesses; the generals who are with us today, our very own generals of today, both black and white cultures running together.

There is such a grafting-in taking place in this new era that is empowering and equipping the army of the Lord. It is establishing many in their true identity as ambassadors of heaven, a significant part of the end time army rising to lead the way and take the ground for the Kingdom of God. The heroes of faith in the great cloud of witnesses, and the angelic realm are joining forces with us to see some of the promises of God fulfilled in this current era. There is an honouring and sharing in the generations of prayer, anointing's and mantles in this hour. The power of the generations is being laid hold of, grasped and outworked through us in this era. The ancient keys are activated, releasing divine intergenerational wisdom and strategy into the now for God's glory.

Prayer:

Father, thank you for grafting me into Jesus, thank you for grafting me in to Abraham, and for grafting me into Israel. Thank you Lord that the blessings of Abraham are my blessings, that the blessings of Israel are my blessings. I now claim those blessings and draw them into my life. Release every spiritual blessing into my life Lord, according to your will and your timing. I open myself to receive your every blessing for my life and I thank you for it Lord. Thank you that I am grafted into an inter-generational portal of ancient wisdom, revelation, understanding and blessing. Let it flow in and through me. Thank you that my part here on earth is part of a prolific power plan that connects us to those heroes of faith in the great cloud of witnesses, and that this live connection enables us to draw on the anointing and mantles to fulfill your promises, for your glory Lord.

Decree:

I decree that I am firmly and securely grafted-in to an inter-generational power source of the Godhead.

I decree that your promises will be fulfilled through this inter-generational portal.

I decree that I am an Ambassador of the Kingdom of God. I am empowered and equipped by your Spirit to fulfil my part in your great plan for the greatest awakening and move of God in this era.

In the mighty name of Jesus. Amen!

Footnotes:

(1) Tim Edwards Ministry - Australia, Innisfail, Queensland. Australian Christian Indigenous Apostolic Ministry. Facebook: Tim Edwards Ministry

(2) A portion of this was inspired by Dr Brian Simmons 'The Passion Translation' text or footnotes.

(3) Dutch Sheets Give Him 15: February 2, 2021 Agreeing With The Cloud of Witnesses

Note: the encounter I had of being 'grafted-in' that took place in Australia was around one year after the encounter of being 'grafted-in' that took place in Israel

First Nations people have a deep connection to land.
I felt a deep connection to the land in Israel that was similar to the strong connection to Country I have in my homeland Gomeroi country.

Chapter 4

Heal the Land

14 if my people, who are called by my name, will
humble themselves and pray and seek my face and
turn from their wicked ways, then I will hear from
heaven, and I will forgive their sin and will heal their
land. (2 Chronicles 7:14 NIV).

19 Repent, then, and turn to God, so that your sins
may be wiped out, that times of refreshing may come
from the Lord, (Acts 3:19 NIV).

12 that at that time you were without Christ, being
aliens from the commonwealth of Israel and
strangers from the covenants of promise, having no
hope and without God in the world. 13 But now in
Christ Jesus you who once were far off have been
brought near by the blood of Christ.

14 For He Himself is our peace, who has made both
one, and has broken down the middle wall of
separation, 15 having abolished in His flesh the
enmity, that is, the law of commandments contained
in ordinances, so as to create in Himself one new
man from the two, thus making peace, 16 and that
He might reconcile them both to God in one body
through the cross, thereby putting to death the
enmity. (Ephesians 2:12-16 NKJV)

(2 Chronicles 7:14 NIV; Acts 3:19 NIV; Ephesians 2:12-16 NKJV)

My husband and I have been privileged to see Jesus minister inner healing through us to the heart of our nation and to many Pastors, leaders, congregations, churches, gatherings and communities in our own nation of Australia, and throughout Nepal, and The Philippines for many years yielding many testimonies of how Jesus transformed lives through deliverance, healing, restoration and Holy Spirit empowering.

While individuals can have their hearts wounded by trauma and abuse, I believe a nation can also carry wounds. I believe Australia carries a wound in the heart of the nation that needs healing.

Many of our First nation's people of the land and our Non-Indigenous family and friends have been wounded. Where there is a wound, there is pain. The pain has run deep through the generations and through the veins and layers of the land.

The Voices of the land are being called forth, the Tiddas are rising, and I believe the earth is groaning under the birthing pains to bring forth an ancient plan for the nations in this era. To deliver the ancient sound rising from the land. To birth the plans of heaven for nations through the First Nations people of the earth. The earth is groaning, the birthing brings forth fruits of ancient wisdom, first fruits of ancient blessings, and unclaimed blessings from generations ago. This type of birthing brings healing and healing of the land.

While I am speaking of Australia, I believe this is true and applies to other people groups and nations too. So please, take by faith whatever resonates with your Spirit, knowing full well that Jehovah Rapha the Lord God our healer is healing our land and healing the soul wounds of the people, including our First Nations and Non-Indigenous people. Healing promotes the ability to join forces to be one force to be reckoned with.

There is a heritage and an inheritance assigned to our nation and it is an all-inclusive Kingdom inheritance for every tongue, tribe, language and nation.

Healing of the Land

The idea that the land carries wounds and needs healing may be a new concept to some people.

In the chapter 'Grafted In' I shared my encounter in the Garden of Gethsemane in Jerusalem. My husband and I were in the Garden and suddenly I was taken into a timeless encounter. It was as if I was experiencing, in a small way, what had taken place in the Garden. I was experiencing a glimpse of the memories locked up in land from 2000 years ago. It seemed that my Spirit's interconnectedness to the spirituality of the Holy Land spanned the generational timelines.

When Stacey Campbell (a highly respected prophet from the USA) saw me after this encounter, while I was still experiencing the effects of it, she said four words to me that impacted me in a profound way. She said 'it's an Indigenous thing.'

She recognised First Nations connectedness to the land. These four words released a floodgate of healing that surged like a river through the cells of my body and the fibers of my being. Just as the blood of Jesus surges through the deep layers of the land, cleansing and releasing it from the effects of its lodged trauma, her words activated the same for me.

While she wasn't experiencing the same thing, she knew and understood the Spiritual connectedness we as First Nations people have with the land.

It was so powerful and I am overcome yet again writing about this.

I want to now establish a biblical foundation for human interaction with the land. This is part of our innate being as First Nations people. For First Nation people there is a connection to land and country that is different to some other cultures.

In Genesis 4 when Cain killed Abel, the Lord said to Cain:

> *"Where is your brother Abel? ... What have you done? ... Your brother's blood cries out to me from the ground...* God then declared a curse on the land as a result of Cain's sin, and said, *"When you work the ground, it will no longer yield its crops for you"* (v 9-12 NIV).

To me, these verses illustrate two things, first the land has memory and the sins of the people are retained by the land and cry out to God for justice. Second, the sins of the people bring a curse on the land which means the land is no longer fruitful or able to bring forth a prosperous harvest.

In Deuteronomy 28 when God detailed the blessings and curses associated with obedience and disobedience, He said if you will obey me I will bless the crops of your land (vs 4), however if you disobey me, your baskets and kneading bowl will be cursed, and the crops of your land will be cursed (vs18).

Why are the crops blessed and cursed according to the obedience and disobedience of the people? Because their obedience or disobedience resulted in the land being blessed or cursed. These are irrevocable laws of creation that have existed since creation. Our interaction and activity on the land leaves a generational footprint of blessing or cursing.

We read in 2 Chronicles:

> *"If My people who are called by My name, will humble themselves and pray and seek My face, and turn from their wicked ways, then I will hear from heaven, and I will forgive their sin and will heal their land. (7:14 NIV)*

When we as the people of God humble ourselves, repent, pray seek His face and turn from our wicked ways of the world, God forgives us and then heals the land.

In Romans 8 we read:

> *"For the creation waits in eager expectation for the children of God to be revealed. For the creation was subjected to frustration, not by its own choice, but by the will of the one who subjected it, in hope that the creation itself will be liberated from its bondage to decay and brought into the freedom and glory of the children of God.*

We know that the whole creation has been groaning as in the pains of childbirth right up to the present time". (See vs 19-22 NIV).

Paul speaks of a creation that is 'subject to frustration', 'in bondage to decay' and 'groaning as in the pains of childhood right up to the present time'. It is waiting for the Sons of God to arise and be revealed. When they arise creation will be 'liberated from its bondage to decay' and will enter into the 'freedom and glory of the Sons of God'. As the Sons of God go, so does creation, whether into cursing and bondage, or blessing and liberty. Then in Mark's version of the Great Commission is, 'Go into all the world (cosmos) and preach the Gospel to all creation' (Mk 16:15). I believe the Gospel and the atoning work of Christ not only effects humanity, it has implications for 'all creation', the entire cosmos and this includes the land.

First Nation people and Land

Many First Nations people believe creation is a part of us as a human race, and we are a part of creation. The way I see it, is that God created the earth and all things in it. Then He formed man from the dust of the land/earth and breathed life into his nostrils. We are formed from the dust of the land, we are part of the land and the land is a part of us. The true essence of who we are is Spirit. We are Spirit being, life breathed into us from God and we have the Spirit of God in us. However our physical being is formed from the dust of the earth.

For many First Nations people, we see ourselves as Custodians of the land, with responsibility to care for the land and bless the land. We are to steward the land well, just as we are custodians of what the Spirit of the Lord is saying to us and to the Church, we are to also called to be custodians of and steward what the Lord is speaking to us well. When entrusted with the knowledge and responsibility to care for the land, this provides a deep sense of identity, purpose and belonging. God gave us dominion over the fish of the sea, over the birds of the air and over every living thing that moves on the earth (see Genesis 1:28 NKJV). This deep relationship between people and the land is often described as 'connection to Country'. (See 'appendix' for more information regarding 'On Country').

The Wound in the Land

A lot of cursing and killing, stealing and destroying happened on Country and across the land of Australia by both our First Nation ancestors and Non- Aboriginal forefathers. The sin committed by people on Country yields a harvest of the bad seed sown.

As we stand together, black and white united in the Spirit of repentance, reconciliation and partnership with Holy Spirit, we exercise our authority as brothers and sisters with the same Father, and as sons and Daughters of the King of all Kings to break the age old cursing and call forth the land to yield a harvest that speaks a better word. To command the land to yield a harvest of the generations of prayer and travail, and the preaching of the word of God. To stand together in the power of agreement. To command the land to yield blessing instead of cursing.

Isaiah 35 highlights what the healing of the land looks like. *"The deserts and the parched land will be glad, the wilderness will rejoice and blossom. Like the crocus, it will burst into bloom, it will rejoice greatly and shout for joy. The glory of Lebanon will be given to it, the splendor of Carmel and Sharon, they will see the glory of the Lord and the splendor of Sharon"* (vs 1, 2).

These verses highlight firstly the contrast between "deserts and parched lands", and the land full of blossom and plant life. Secondly the verses tell us, the land "rejoices greatly" and "shouts for joy", and the "glory of the Lord" will be seen in the land. When the land rejoices the people rejoice. When the land is under a curse the people also live under the curse of a land that doesn't yield a prosperous harvest.

Isaiah 55 speaks of, *"You will go out in joy and be led forth in peace; the mountains and hills will burst into song before you, and all the trees of the field will clap their hands. Instead of the thornbush will grow the juniper, and instead of briers the myrtle will grow. This will be for the LORD's renown, for an everlasting sign, that will endure forever* (Vs 12, 13).

Imagine the mountains bursting into song, and the trees of the field clapping their hands.

This is a creation liberated by the arising of the sons of God

God wants to heal and bless our land, so the people of the land operate in blessing and abundance. The land however has a memory of iniquity that goes back generations. The curse on the land may not be because of the behavior of this generation, it may be the result of the iniquity of past generations of all cultures and nations that have lived in this land.

Let me now apply this to the land of Australia. The land in the Nation of Australia still bears the effects of a wound, and that wound cries out to the Lord, just as the blood of Abel cried out to the Lord.

The answer is the atoning blood of Jesus.

 And we have come to Jesus who established a new covenant with his blood sprinkled upon the mercy seat; blood that continues to speak from heaven, "forgiveness," a better message than Abel's blood that cries from the earth, "justice." (See Hebrews 12:24 TPT)

Encounter:

Last night, I believe the Lord allowed me to experience a tiny glimpse of the greater pain in our nation, that our First Nations people live with. I felt extreme pressure on my chest, I was pulling back my clothes, in an attempt to breathe. I felt like I was about to have a heart attack.

I knew it wasn't mine. I was experiencing what had been released into the atmosphere over our nation, a Spirit of death manifesting through a Spirit of oppression, fear, anger. The oppression I felt was suffocating. I was struggling to breathe and the pain was searing. It was crushing. I had to immediately begin to decree the word of God, to push back the powers of darkness.

My husband and I were taken into a place of intercession for the protection, healing and well-being of our Nation, and our First Nations people. As we interceded, the pressure, the pain, and the oppression began to lift.

The message that resounded was this: Intercessors, Gate Keepers and Watchman Warriors please take your place and pray. You have authority to overturn the plans of the enemy in this hour.

Prayer to Heal the Wound in the Heart of a Nation, the People and the Heart of the Land

Father, we ask you to remove the trauma, remove the pain, and remove the fear, the shock, and the terror resulting from the wound in the heart of our people and the heart of our land. Lord you take the pain from the Spirit, Soul and Body of our First Nations people. Lord, we give you the pain. Father, heal the heart of our nation Lord, heal the hearts of our First Nations people, and heal the hearts of all people in our nation Lord.

Pour out your anointing and your healing balm, to flow through the chambers of our hearts, to flow through the heart of the land of our nation Lord. Let it flow like a river, releasing healing through the power of the blood of Jesus to flow powerfully through our people, and through the Body of Christ. Bringing healing to the bodies of the First Nations people. Heal their bodies, right down to the cellular level Lord God. Release your people from age old diseases and sicknesses that have lodged in the body and travelled through the generations.

Dislodge sicknesses, dislodge diabetes, dislodge renal failure, we say pancreas be restored, kidneys re-create in creative miracles in Jesus name. We speak life over our nation. We speak to the heart of our nation and we say be revived in Jesus name.

Father, release healing into the **soul realm**. Heal the emotions, nervous systems be restored and healed now as we pray this prayer. Anxiety be gone. Fear be gone, pour out the perfect love of the Father that drives out all fear in Jesus name.

Go back through the years of the generations Lord, release the healing power of God into every year of every generation. I speak the name of Jehovah Rapha, the Lord God our healer into the heart of our nation, and say *revive, revive.*

Release healing to every crushed Spirit and broken body, every hurt heart in our nation. Miraculously remove the scars, restore the hearts of our First Nations people, and restore the heart of our nation to beat as ONE with the heart of the Father. Every tongue, every tribe, every nation and generation, we call you into alignment with the ONE heartbeat, the heartbeat of the Father. In one accord, with one voice, one heart. I declare unity and oneness over our nation, in Jesus name.

Restore the foundation of our Nation:

Break the power of the lies set in the foundation of our Nation. Break all its destructive effects, back through the generations. Replace, rebuild, and re-construct it with the *truth* of your word, the truth that sets our nation free.

Lord tell the person reading this 'what is your truth? the truth that breathes new life, resurrection life into them. Breathe on us Holy Spirit, the fresh breath of God. Release the wind of the Holy Spirit across our lands, in Jesus mighty name, Amen. We, as a nation have an opportunity right before us. It is an opportunity to release the heart of the Father into this nation.

To see the heart of forgiveness and the justice heart of Father God pour out like a river. A river that flows through the land and heart of our nation, bringing healing, restoration, refreshing, reformation and transformation.
Together, with one another and with Holy Spirit, I believe we can release Fathers heart in a stunning way.

We don't have to understand everything that is happening, but we can respond by pouring out the love of God on one another. Love that honours, love like healing balm to our land and our nation.

Our response as believers, as Sons and Daughters, and as Mothers and Fathers in this nation, to a hurting nation will represent how the world, how our brothers and sisters, and how our families and communities, see the Church and how they ultimately see Jesus through us.

What an opportunity we have to shine the love and the light of Jesus into this darkness that is trying to cover the earth. We have an opportunity to partner with Holy Spirit to heal a nation. To bring reformation and transformation in this era. Pray for God to raise up the reformers with a heart of wisdom and a heart of love. Intercessors, gate keepers, and watchman warriors this is the hour to rise up in prayer and intercession, decreeing the word of the Lord to see our nation *arise and shine*.

Let us decree: Australia Arise and Shine, for your light has come and the Glory of the Lord has risen upon you. Amen!

I encourage you to make this decree over your nation, wherever you are in the world. I believe Isaiah 60 is relevant to the times we are in, as the darkness of COVID and the darkness of oppression, the darkness of fear and the darkness of trauma attempts to cover the earth. I also believe that Isaiah 61 can help us navigate these times.

Communion: For Healing of the Land

At this point in these writings, I would like to invite you to get ready to take communion from wherever you are in the world. To join your heart with many other believers to see the power of the blood of Jesus bring healing to the land, healing to the people of the land and healing to you personally. Jesus shed his blood on the cross for us to live a prosperous life and in good health. Take a moment right now to get your communion elements ready. There will be an opportunity for you, towards the end of this chapter, to join the many others across this nation and other nations who took part in a powerful nation-wide communion.

To provide some background information for taking communion over the land, let me share with you about the National Solemn Assembly held in 2020. (1)

National Solemn Assembly

I have the honour to share with you about a National gathering of many thousands of people from many tribes, nations, generations and denominations from Australia, New Zealand, Israel, America and other global networks who joined hearts and united for a National Solemn Assembly in Australia on 26-27 September, in 2020.

A very powerful and moving moment in time. It was an historic moment for the nation. There was a profound shift over the nation that changed the course of a nation toward the healing of the land and the advancement of the Kingdom of God in the nation and the nations.

Pastor Peter Walker, his wife Ps Maria Walker and Ps Tim Edwards, First Nations Apostolic National Leaders led this Solemn Assembly alongside Warwick and Alison Marsh of National Day of Prayer and Fasting;

and Bishop Philip Huggins the President of the National Council of Churches. There were many other highly respected National Apostles and leaders who were part of the leadership team and played a significant role in this National Solemn Assembly.

The National Solemn Assembly (NSA) is a movement, led by the Australian First Nations Christian Apostles and leaders, alongside leaders of the National Day of Prayer and Fasting in Australia, and joined by various highly respected Non Indigenous Christian leaders. It is aimed at facilitating release, restoration and wholeness across our land and nation.

'This is a call to all Australians and other Indigenous Elders and people who call this country home to come together on-line or in-person in unity and oneness – to seek God's face according to 2 Chronicles 7:13-14, and Joel 1:14 for the healing of the land. It is for all Australians to unite with one voice in prayer for repentance, forgiveness and reconciliation to God and one another.' (1)

Thank you to Ps Peter and Maria Walker, Ps Tim Edwards, Warwick Marsh, Bishop Phillip Huggins and the many other Christian leaders who made this a reality. What an honour and privilege it was for me to take part in this leading out in prayer and being given a short speaking spot to lead us all in one of the communion times.

Communion Opportunity:

During the Solemn Assembly I had the privilege and honour to give a short communion message to the National Solemn Assembly. It was a real honour to bring communion at such an historic and significant time in history.

On this day we joined as one body, one voice, and one Kingdom family. Now I would like to share an adapted version of that message with you and invite you to join me to take communion to bring forth healing in the land:

Today I would like to share about the power of the broken body and shed blood of Jesus. The power this has in our own lives and the power of it in this hour for us corporately across a nation and the nations. When we apply the power of the blood of Jesus to the land in our nation, I believe healing will arise in our nation, as the Son, the risen King rises with healing in His wings.

The Power of the Broken Body and the Blood of Jesus

The shed blood of Jesus and His broken body has the power to:
- Power to save the most hardened heart of a sinner into a Son or Daughter, a saint
- Power to get deep down into our wound, cleanse it, purify the chambers of our heart and to completely heal the pain, and restore us as new, as if we had never been wounded.
- On a national scale, there is power in the blood of Jesus to heal every disease and infirmity in every person on earth.
- Its power reaches across timelines and generations, past, present and future. All the way back to redeem Adam and all the way into the future to redeem the last baby to be born.
- It has the power to break chains of bondage, to deliver us, and to set the most oppressed person free!

\-   Its power is able to break every generational curse over every nation in the earth and release generational blessings for future generations to come!

The blood of Jesus is infinitely powerful. It is as alive and powerful today, as it was when Jesus shed His blood 2000 years ago.

Our Participation in the Blood

> *1 **Corinthians 10:16 (NIV) 16** Is not the cup of thanksgiving (the blood) for which we give thanks a participation in the blood of Christ? And is not the bread that we break (Jesus body) - **a participation in** the body of Christ?*

Today when we take the communion elements, the bread and the wine, we are participating in the body and blood of the Lord Jesus, in all its resurrection power.

Jesus said in John 6 (NIV)

We are participating in the power of His resurrection

> *Verse* [31] *Our ancestors ate the manna in the wilderness; as it is written: 'He gave them bread from heaven to eat.' (John 6:31 NIV). So God gave them the manna to eat*

Jesus went on to say it's not Moses who gives you bread from heaven, it's my Father who gives you *true bread from heaven.* This bread gives life to the world.

That's Jesus! Jesus gives life. He gave His life and He still gives life today.

Paraphrasing, Jesus says in verse 53 unless you eat the flesh of the Son of Man (Jesus) and drink his blood, you have no life in you. But when you do, you have eternal life, and you remain in me and I remain in you. There is a demonstration of oneness right there between you and Jesus.

> Verse [58] *This is the bread that came down from heaven. Your ancestors ate manna and died, but whoever feeds on this bread from heaven will live forever."* (John 6:58 NIV)
>
> In 1 Corinthians 11:23 Jesus took the bread gave thanks, broke it and said, *"this is my body", v25 then he took the cup and said "this is my blood".* (CEV)

When we participate in communion we are participating in the full power of the cross, and in the power of his life changing blood, and in the power of his broken body. In the physical realm this is just bread and wine, in the spirit realm these elements are the blood and body of Christ.

Jesus said, whoever eats my flesh and drinks my blood remains in me. At an individual level, by taking these elements we participate in the power of the blood and body of Jesus, this makes the way for sickness to be healed, chains to be broken off, sin patterns broken, and God's life and power to flow through us. It is an ancient generational covenant and connection that spans all timelines.

The Blood Applied Nationally

We read in Genesis where the innocent blood of Abel cried out for justice

> (In Gen 4:10) "The Lord said to Cain, *"your brother's blood cries out to me from the ground"* (NIV)

What we learn from this verse is that blood has a voice, and Abel's innocent blood was crying out for justice.

I believe the voice of our ancestor's blood and the blood shed caused by our ancestor's in our lands - is crying out across our nation and the nations today. It's a voice that reaches our spiritual ears and resounds in our heart and Spirit, and it reaches to heaven – can you hear it? It's calling for Justice, we call for righteousness, and the call is for healing of the land.

Let me highlight right here that:

In Hebrews 12:24 (NIV) we read:

> *"To Jesus the mediator of a new covenant, and to the sprinkled blood that speaks a better word than the blood of Abel"*

The blood of Jesus speaks a better word! Today we come into agreement with the better word over our nation. We repent on behalf of our forefathers for all blood guilt sin and all bloodshed, by our First Nation ancestors and by our Non-Indigenous ancestors. We break the power of a wrong and ungodly covenant and break the curse that came upon the land as a result. We come out of agreement with a wrong covenant and come into agreement with the new covenant. The new covenant, that by the sprinkled blood of Jesus that speaks a better word over our nation.

Jesus is the voice of righteousness and justice. Jesus blood is a powerful answer to the curses on our nations because of innocent blood shed.

As we repent, as one body together for the past sins of our nation, (both the sins of our First Nations forefathers and the sins of our Non-Indigenous forefathers), then the blood of Jesus will satisfy the cry coming out of the land.

We have been repenting as one body, one voice in this Solemn Assembly. Let's believe together, as we get ready to take communion, that the blood of Jesus is powerful to bring healing to the wound in our nation and bring healing to the heart of our nation. Let us believe together that in doing this, Jesus brings healing to the land of our nation.

Jesus bore the sins of the nation and he also became a curse.

The Bible says:

> *"Christ redeemed us from the curse of the Law, having become a curse for us—for it is written, "Cursed is everyone who hangs on a tree"* (Galatians 3:13 NASB). It was done at the Cross.

Jesus bore our sin and bore the consequence of our sin, the curse of the law, by becoming a curse for us and the whole of every nation.

Take the Elements

As we take communion and remember Jesus at the Cross, lets apply Jesus' blood and body to our own life in faith, to receive the cleansing, the restoration and healing to our bodies, deliverance from sin and addictions, and/or demonic bondages that we may need to be released from.

Let us also take it, believing that Jesus blood is powerful in our nation of Australia and all nations to satisfy the cry for righteousness and justice for and from the innocent blood shed in generations past. It is powerful to lift the curses over our land in the present here and now, and we receive the generational blessing of God to flow out into our future and the blessed future of our restored and reformed nation.

Jesus took the bread, gave thanks and said this is my body, which is broken for you, take and eat. In like manner He took the wine and said this is my blood.

Thank you for the power of your broken body Jesus. Thank you for the power of your blood Jesus, to break the strongholds over our lives and over our nation, to heal and restore the soul wounds in us and to heal and restore the wound in the land of our beloved nation and nations.

Release your healing power through the chambers of our heart, our bodies, our soul and our Spirit. Release the mighty healing power to flow through the veins and the deep layers of our land.

Lord we remember you, your fierce heart of compassion, and your dedicated life to the fulfillment of prophecy in obedience to Father. Jesus we take you into ourselves, in all your glory, in all your healing power and authority. We glorify you, Jesus be glorified in this moment in time. Be glorified in and through us to the world around us. In your mighty name Jesus! Amen.

Now let us take the elements in faith believing that the blood of Jesus is purging unrighteousness from the land and bringing righteousness, peace and joy into the heart of the nation as it brings healing to our land. Let us now eat and drink together.

Encounter:

The day before the Solemn Assembly I had an encounter with the Lord. The Spirit of travailing hit me for this time of Solemn Assembly over our nation. There was a strong sense of the Spirit of the Lord rising over our nation. I could see in the Spirit a huge tidal wave forming, leading up to Solemn Assembly. Zechariah 4:6 Not by might, nor by power but by my spirit says the Lord of Hosts (NKJV).

As the tidal wave broke forth on the land, I saw the heavens over our nation, instantly break open – creating an open heaven over our nation – a large portal of heaven over Australia. The tidal wave broke and flooded the waterways, and river ways from coast to the desert lands. I saw streams in the desert, it caused the seeds laying dormant, the seeds in waiting to spring up and flourish, and these are soul seeds in waiting. They are souls. It led to a great harvest of souls. We declare Salvation over our nation. The landscape was transformed. The wasteland was reformed. The reformation of the landscape began.

The tidal wave on impact caused a deep surge down into the layers of the land. It was like the *very blood of Jesus* was at work loosing ancient old strongholds. The evil intent was made null and void. It released the generational trauma that had lodged in the land, and healing of the land began. The surge purged the land, deep down through the deepest layers.

As it broke the generational curses, it released healing through the generations, and the promise of generational blessings, which flowed and flooded over the land.

 Abundance was released over our nation.

Prayer to Release the Encounter:

Jesus, through the power of your blood and broken body for us, I ask that you release the tidal wave of the Spirit of God, the love of God to break forth and break into our hearts and into the land of our nation.

As this tidal wave hits the ground, Lord cause there to be an instant breaking open of the heavens over this nation. Release a surge of your perfect love that drives out all fear, a surge of your healing power to flood the dry parched land of our nation.

As the resurrection Spirit of God floods across the waterways, river ways and land, cause the seeds laying dormant, the souls laying dormant *to come alive* and *come to life*. 'Soul Seeds in Waiting,' we say spring up in Salvation across this nation. We command the land to yield its harvest from the seed of intercession and prayers sown.

The surge of the *love of* God into the land, causes a deep breaking open of the ground, as the Spirit of the living God travels deep into the land, releasing the *power of the blood of Jesus* to break ancient old strongholds lodged in our land. It removes the generations of generational trauma from the land and our people. Release the healing power of the cross - deep into the layers of the land and deep into our souls.

Break the generational curses and release generational blessings to spring up with new life and launch us forth into abundance. Lord release the tidal wave of revival and reformation over our nation. Let flames of fire ride on the wave as it crashes in. Release flames of fire in the flood to spread through our land. Set us ablaze with revival fire that will see transformation of the landscape take shape, as it yields its great harvest.

Sow transformation in our hearts, and transformation in the heart of our nation as it is flooded with the supernatural new dimensions of the LOVE of God.

Let this tidal wave cause a *'heart transplant'* for this nation, to beat and dance to a new rhythm, as the waters of life flow throughout the land. We decree reformation of the nation. In your mighty name, Yeshua Ha mashiach!

Prayer Points for the Nation:
(As per objectives for National Solemn Assembly 2020)

- Pray for a National Awakening that will bring Revival, Reformation and Transformation to Australia.
- Foster forgiveness, healing, and unity.
- Curses broken off the peoples and the land, giving rise to opportunity and productivity as a token of God's blessing.
- Restoration of all Australian and Indigenous people into their God-ordained purposes and destiny (Joel 2:25)

Establish righteousness and justice across all the land, irrespective of race or creed.

Reformation of Godliness throughout our communities and government, throughout all Australia, to enter our destiny as the Great Southland of the Holy Spirit.

Footnotes:
(1) https://www.nationaldayofprayer.org.au/solemn-assembly/

NATIONAL SOLEMN ASSEMBLY www.nationaldayofprayer.org.au/Solemn-Assembly. NATIONAL Solemn. Assembly. "For the Healing of the Land". 26 - 27 September 2020.

(2) Peter and Katherine Dunstan 'Healing Wounded Hearts' amazon.com.au
(3) Resource Indigenous Perspectives (Res005 Mar 2008)

APPENDIX:

On Country

The term "Country" or 'On Country' is often used by our First Nations people to describe our family origins and associations with particular parts of Australia. For example, I am a Gomeroi (Goh-merr-roy) woman from North-Western NSW, the Mooki (Mook-eye) River area is my Country or I am an Allen Sampson from Gomeroi Country.

First Nations people have traditionally utilised plants, animals and other natural materials from the Australian environment, showing a distinct relationship to country. These resources met, and for some still meet basic human needs for First Nation Australians — such as food, shelter, clothing and medicines — but have also been used to create tools, weapons, art, craft and ceremonial objects.

Within traditional First Nation Aboriginal societies, each Indigenous language group has a defined area of land or country that each group is connected to, both geographically and spiritually. An estimated 700 language groups across Australia once contributed to a diverse mix of cultures, stories and relationships, all specific to areas of land and the environment people lived and travelled. Today, the First Nation Indigenous Australians have strong connection to country. Over thousands of years, the environmental practices of Aboriginal people and Torres Strait Islander people led to an ecologically sustainable way of life for many communities. ('Relationships to country: Aboriginal people and Torres Strait Islander people' Res005 Mar 2008).

Website: www.qsa.qld.edu.au Page 2 of 2 Res005 Mar 2008

Chapter 5

Lift and Shift

For we share in one faith, one baptism, and one
Father.

(Ephesians 4:5 TPT)

"Children of God through faith, for all of you who were
baptized into Christ have clothed yourselves with
Christ. There is neither Jew nor Gentile, neither slave
nor free, nor is there male and female, for you are all
one in Christ Jesus. If you belong to Christ, then you
are Abraham's seed, and heirs according to the
promise".

(Galatians 3:26-29 NIV)

I am excited about my prayer day at the Gara Gorge, part of the Oxley Wild Rivers National Park, NSW Australia. I love, love, love these times with my Lord. Prayer is our lifestyle, but there is something really special about going to an old favourite spot where you have had so many wonderful encounters with the Lord while reading and meditating on His word.

Today there was a profound sense that the Lord was beginning to download an apostolic blueprint and God strategy for our nation of Australia. There was a sobering weightiness in the atmosphere that caused every member of my being to fall at the feet of Jesus. I was truly in a state of wonder and anticipation of what Father was about to reveal. The reverential fear of the Lord God Almighty and the sovereignty of God was all over me.

The Lord was delivering to me a national word for Australia; Indigenous and Non-Indigenous Australia, the Australian Bride of Christ.

This day, I felt the pouring out of Father's love for our Nation Australia, First Nations and Non-Indigenous alike. It poured out like a powerful waterfall. God was showing me our Nation of Australia, as He had been for a while. He spoke to me from two perspectives and showed me how He was calling His people to become one.

First Nations Boundary Lines

First He showed me the map of Indigenous Australia. This is a map of the many First Nations clan groups in the land of Australia. There are over 500 Aboriginal Nations in Australia.

I am a Gomeroi (Gohm-err-oi) woman from the North West Slopes region of NSW, Australia, near the Mooki (Mook-eye) River. If you look closely on the below map, you can see Kamilaroi (Guh-mill-arr-oi) / Gomeroi (Gohm-err-oi) Country in NSW. It's the second largest Indigenous footprint in the state of NSW. You might hear it referred to as Kamilaroi, Gomeroi, Gamilaroi (Ga-mill-uh-rroi), and Gamilaraay (Ga-mill-uh-ray). These are all name variations of the same geographical location.

Our culture is an oral one and traditionally, we have passed down stories, teachings, and learn through oral methods and not written ways. So our Gamilaraay/Gomeroi language was not traditionally written down. Today the language has been revived and is thriving and active to varying degrees in different locations.

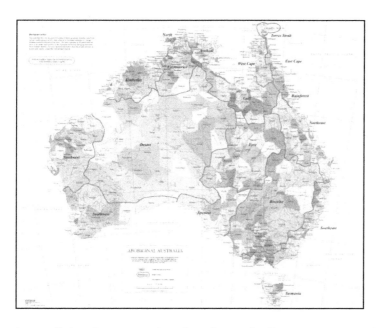

https://aiatsis.gov.au/explore/map-indigenous-australia

This is a Map of the many First Nations country lands within Australia. Each one has its own name. For instance my country is Kamilaroi on this map. We pronounce it Gamilaroi or Gomeroi.

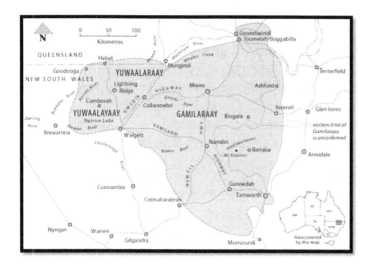

Maps of Gamilaraay/Yuwaalaraay countrydnathan.com
Gamilaraay Country is also known as Kamilaroi, Gamilaroi, or Gomeroi
Country. These are slightly different pronunciations for the same land
mass.

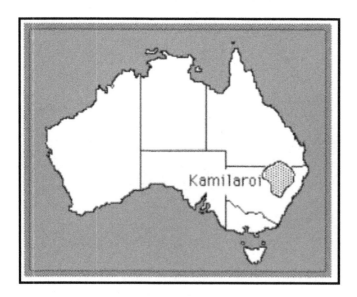

Location - Kamilaroi - A Nations Identity
kamilaroinationsidentity.weebly.com
Kamilaroi Country is highlighted here in this map in the State of NSW on
the map of Australia.

Location - Kamilaroi - A Nations Identity kamilaroianationsidentity.weebly

Close up of Kamilaroi Country in amongst other Indigenous nations on this segment of the map of Australia.

Removing Spiritual Separation

In my encounter, the Lord highlighted to me the boundary lines outlining every Indigenous nation. What He did with them was powerful! Right before my eyes He welded every border together into *one* steel framework. It was all one piece. It was a framework set in place.

I had a strong sense that the Lord wanted to lift the framework of boundary lines. In this particular vision they represented spiritual barriers causing conflict between First Nations people groups and barriers and factions that separate our First Nation peoples from other Indigenous nations in Australia.

I would like to say that the Lord was not wanting to remove our Godly cultural values, kinship or our identity as First Nations people. He created us especially as First Nation people for His wonderful Kingdom purposes. We honour the diversity of our First Nations people.

This was a supernatural removing of spiritual barriers. The Lord has a grand plan for First Nations people to lead as a united people group, with Christ. For us to be empowered, by the power of the Holy Spirit, with Kingdom blueprints, plans and purposes to set the nations ablaze with revival fires. This is part of the new sound rising from the land.

The welding together of all the boundary lines into one, signified that the Lord wanted to remove 'division and separation'. This was to allow a uniting of all Indigenous nations across the Country and to put an end to factions in communities. To unite our Indigenous nations for His Kingdom purposes in this era. To *lift and shift* the barriers so that the 'River of Unity' would freely flow right across the land amongst all First Nations tribes and language groups.

It wasn't to take our unique cultural attributes away. No, God is celebrating and championing the unique design He crafted for our people. By uniting like this, we strengthen one another. It will be like an expansion of kinship and community in a powerful way.

The purpose is to come into Kingdom Unity. It was as if there was a call to:

> "Awaken, arise, and come into one accord for My Kingdom purposes".

I felt the Lord's heart for His people. He is inviting us to draw near to Him so He can get even closer to us (see James 4:8). It is here in this intimate place that He can reveal His heart for us as a people group, as a nationality, and as a country.

Non-Indigenous Border Lines

It didn't stop there. In my encounter the Lord and I looked again and this time, He showed me other boundary lines causing separation in the nation. The border lines of each State and Territory of Australia that had been established by our Non-Indigenous Australian brothers and sisters. These are the borders and boundaries of NSW, QLD, Northern Territory, Western Australia, South Australia, Tasmania, ACT and Victoria.

Lists 190 & 489 By States – AXYN axyn.com.au
Australian States including Australian Capital Territory (ACT) where our nation's Capital Canberra is situated.

In the encounter the Lord proceeded to weld these boundary lines together into one framework. In this part of the vision, this framework was placed on top of the framework of the map of Indigenous nations.

Becoming One Australian Bride

So now we were looking at the map of Australia and it had the Indigenous boundary lines welded together into one frame. It also had the State and Territory boundary lines welded together into another frame.

The Lord then took both of these frames and welded the Indigenous and the Non-Indigenous frameworks together into the final piece, one framework.

So we had one steel framework of both Indigenous and Non-Indigenous borders. Again, there was a sense of the Lord wanting to lift the spiritual borders that separated His people. I can also sense the longing of the Fathers heart to see all His children together in unity.

For all to live and move and have their beings in the one, true living Father God of all nations across the earth. Again I sense a call to:

> 'Awaken, arise, and come into one accord for My Kingdom purposes.'

> *Now the God who raised up our Lord from the grave will **awaken** and raise us up through his mighty power!* (1 Corinthians 6:14 TPT)

While you and I come "*from every nation, tribe, people and language* (see Rev 7:9) when we are grafted into Christ (see Rom 6:2-5) and enter the Kingdom of God, we all became as Galatians 3:26-29 says:

> *"Children of God through faith, for all of you who were baptized into Christ have clothed yourselves with Christ. There is neither Jew nor Gentile, neither slave nor free, nor is there male and female, for you are all one in Christ Jesus. If you belong to Christ, then you are Abraham's seed, and heirs according to the promise".* (Galatians 3:26-29 NIV)

God in Christ has translated us from the Kingdom of this world into the Kingdom of His Son (see Rev 11:15). We have all come into the *family of God*. In the Kingdom of God and the family of God there are no Spiritual borders separating us, and there are no geographical boundaries and borders, no steel framework.

Then He did this in the encounter: He took the whole framework in one piece and He *popped it off the land*! The Lord was speaking loudly to me – *Borders and barriers LIFT AND SHIFT!*

Such a profound sense of freedom surrounded me. The land was free! The people were free! Free to love one another and free to love God. No more factions within our First Nations tribes. No more divisive spirit running rampart in our nation.

I believe The Lord is *Removing Spiritual Separation* in this nation! Amen! So that the 'River of Unity' will freely flow with the SPIRIT of GOD, right across this land.

The thought that comes to mind is that it will be like a *supernatural force of unstoppable unity*.

In the Spirit realm, I sense that the Lord is removing divisive heart attitudes, barriers, blockages, and man-made borders that keep His people from joining and flowing in the *one* Spirit of God as *one warrior bride*.

For we share in one faith, one baptism, and one Father. (Ephesians 4:5 TPT)

Now I'm not saying that we are going to lose our unique attributes – no – the Lord is celebrating the *diverse uniqueness*! It is the *diversity in unity.*

I heard the Lord say:

I am Reclaiming and Reframing My country!

I claim her as MINE!

I Frame her as Family!

The Lord wants to remove all spiritual boundary lines that have been separating His people, black, white or brindle. This is to make way for His Bride, not brides but for one radiant bride to arise.

The Lord spoke again to me:

I am coming back for my Kingdom bride without spot, wrinkle or blemish. Remove the blemish of Disunity. Replace it with My Kingdom Unity.

You and I are invited into this powerful dimension of unity and family oneness! My brothers and sisters I encourage you to prepare your hearts for this.

Diversity in unity. Unity is the battle strategy of Heaven being released right now. Amen!

I believe that as we position ourselves and bring our heart attitude into alignment with the Father's heart of unity, God is setting us up to reap a harvest of the miraculous, an outpouring of the supernatural, and miracles in a magnitude unthinkable! Are you ready for it? The wave is rising!

Hidden Beneath the Weight of the Separation

Once the framework was removed, during this encounter, it revealed something devastating and yet, I felt great hope at the same time. I could see deep trenches in the landscape where the borders had been. The trenches were filled with the remains of skeletons. It spoke loudly of dead bones.

The Lord took me to The Valley of Dry Bones in Ezekiel 37:1-14.

There is a call to awaken – wake from the dead, to resurrect these bones. That song called 'Awake My Soul' By Chris Tomlin (6) ran in my head as a strong declaration:

> *'Awake, awake, awake my soul-oul,*
> *God resurrect these bones*
> *From death to life*
> *For you alo-one*
> *God resurrect these bones*

Lyrics:
[Chris Tomlin:]
Breathe on me, breath of God, breathe on me
Breathe on me, breath of God, breathe on me
I come alive, I'm alive when You breathe on me
I come alive, I'm alive when You breathe on me

[Chorus:]
Awake, awake, awake my soul,
God resurrect these bones
From death to life, for You alone
Awake my soul

Speak to me, Word of God, speak to me
Speak to me, Word of God, speak to me
I come alive, I'm alive when you speak to me
I come alive, I'm alive when you speak to me

[Chorus:]
Awake, awake, awake my soul,
God resurrect these bones From death to life,
for You alone Awake my soul

[Lecrae:]
Then He said to me,
Prophesy to these bones and say to them,
Dry bones, hear the word of the Lord!
This is what the Sovereign Lord says to these bones,
I will make breath enter you,
And you will come alive.
So I prophesied as I was commanded.
As I was prophesying, there was a noise, a rattling sound,
And the bones came together, bone to bone.
And I looked, and tendons and flesh appeared on them,
And skin covered them, but there was no breath in them.
Then He said to me,
Prophesy to the breath,
Prophesy, son of man, and say to it,
Come from the four winds of breath and breathe.

[Chorus:]
Awake, awake, awake my soul,
God resurrect these bones
From death to life, through you alone
Awake my soul

In the encounter, I was looking at the trenches filled to the brim, with skeletal bones. I was looking at the valley of dry bones in the land of our nation.

I believe there is a call to rise up out of the trenches, to arise and shine.

> *Arise and shine for your light has come and the glory of the Lord rises upon you (Isaiah 60:1).*

I sense the Lord calling to *us come, come to me, watch me open the wells of Salvation in this nation! Arise!*

Out of the Trenches Life Arises

Straight away, in this vision, I saw the trenches fill to the brim with running water. The trenches became a river with fast flowing water dancing throughout our nation.

The Lord spoke to me through song again: this one is called 'In the River' by Jesus Culture (7)

> *We come alive in the river*
> *We come alive in the river*
> *Spring up a well*
>
> *Break open prison doors*
> *Set all the captives free*
> *Spring up a well, spring up a well*
> *Spring up a well in me*
>
> *We come alive in the river*

Oh my heart! Yes Lord! There is such joy on this right here friends!

We speak to the dry bones and we decree you will live and not die. You come alive in the river of life.

We speak to our people who are living like death warmed up and we say:

> *Wake up you living gateways! Lift up your heads, you ageless doors of destiny! Welcome the King of Glory, for He is about to come through you.* (Psalm 24:7 TPT)

> *⁸ You ask, "Who is this Glory-King?"*
> *The Lord, armed and ready for battle,*
> *the Mighty One, invincible in every way!*
> *⁹ So wake up, you living gateways, and rejoice!*
> *Fling wide, you ageless doors of destiny!*
> *Here he comes; the King of Glory is ready to come in.*
> *¹⁰ You ask, "Who is this King of Glory?"*
> *He is the Lord of Victory, armed and ready for battle,*
> *the Mighty One, the invincible commander of heaven's host Yes, he is the King of Glory!* (Psalm 24: 8-10 TPT)

We speak over our nation 'come alive, come alive.'

We decree to the prison doors 'OPEN.'
You, who have been held captive to oppression, you are now SET FREE

You, who have been held captive to depression, you are now SET FREE

You, who have been held captive to isolation, you are now SET FREE

Where the Spirit of the Lord is, there is freedom, there is free-do-om. Yes another song. He speaks to us in spiritual psalms, hymns and songs and we make melody in our hearts to the Lord.

This song is by Jesus Culture and called 'Freedom' (8)

> [16] *Let the word of Christ live in you richly, flooding you with all wisdom. Apply the Scriptures as you teach and instruct one another with the Psalms, and with festive praises, and with prophetic songs given to you spontaneously by the Spirit, so sing to God with all your hearts!* (Colossians 3:16 TPT)

We decree this over Australia! Australia, the Spirit of the Lord is upon you, Australia where the Spirit of the Lord is there is freedom. Australia freedom is upon you!

I strongly sensed that some of the dry bones I was seeing represented Indigenous nations while others were representing each State of Australia and the wider non-Aboriginal community. As I read from Ezekiel, I could clearly see that the Lord was revealing His plan to speak to the dry bones calling them to resurrection life.

I could hear in the Spirit, a really loud rattling like a roar. I knew inside of me, that this rattling of bones spoke of the bones coming together, the nations within the first Nation people groups coming together, and the black and white coming together to form one body. What was forming was the body of Christ in a more powerful way than before. This is a body of Kingdom minded people uniting together as one force, a force to be contended with. The rattling rumble turned into a roar over the nation.

I believe the principalities over our nation have held our people in 'lockdown' keeping us from our Kingdom unity, and from true Kingdom identity as sons and daughters of one Kingdom family for way too long. There are mandates, assignments and mantles waiting for you.

It's time Australia, First Nations Australia it's time.

It says in Ps 24:1-4 (TPT):

Yahweh claims the world as his. Everything and everyone belong to him! ² *He's the one who pushed back oceans to let the dry ground appear, planting firm foundations for the earth.* ³ *Who, then, is allowed to ascend the mountain of Yahweh? And who has the privilege of entering into God's Holy Place?* ⁴ *Those who are clean—whose works and ways are pure,*
whose hearts are true and sealed by the truth, those who never deceive, whose words are sure.

The cry of my heart for you, for me, for all of us, is Psalm 51:10:

Create in me a clean heart, O God; and renew a right spirit within me. (Psalm 51:10 KJV)

This is the God whose heart longs for his people to come into the sacred place of deep intimacy with Him, the one who longs to share the deep secrets of His heart with us. This is the heart of the Father of all, to bring us firmly into unity, including all tongues, tribes, languages and nations. Oh friends, my heart bursts open like a fountain with unspeakable joy at the thought of this.

Australia, and all nations, there is a call to awaken, arise, and unite. Arise together as one united Kingdom army of the Lord.

I believe there will be a greater level of awakening, a call for deep cleansing and thorough purifying to come that will set us up to reap a harvest of the miraculous in a magnitude unthinkable in this new era.

You see, the steel framework, in this encounter, represented many years of ancient old strongholds over the nation. The dry bones lay dormant and crushed under the weight of oppression and deception bearing down on our land. But we prophesy life to the dry bones.

We prophesy to the restricted breath - breath come now, come from the four winds, the North, the South, the East and the West. Come to life, stand up on your feet – you are the vast army of the Lord. Arise!

I decree: You come alive in the river of life and now we call the wells to spring up from within the heart of the nation. We cry out 'Salvation' over our Nation. Australia and the nations, we call you to Salvation, we call families, communities, people groups, towns, cities, and regions to salvation in this nation.

We decree, wells of salvation in our nation open and flow like the river through our lands, through the heart of our people in every part of the land.

I believe the wells are being re-dug and re-opened in this nation. Revival fires will spread like water and the knowledge of the glory of the Lord will spread and fill this land like the waters that cover the sea.

In his book "Local Revivals in Australia" Stuart Piggins (1) proposes that 'local revivals have been frequent in Australian history.' In his research he found references to 71 local revivals in nineteenth century Australia. He says 'And far from being impervious (resistant) to revival, the twentieth century has witnessed more revivals than any previous age.'

One revival that springs to mind is the 'The Pinnacle Pocket Revival' in the Atherton Tablelands in Far North Queensland

Australia. It is told that the Pinnacle Pocket spiritual fire spread to many parts of Australia during the 1960's.

Families moved to other parts of Queensland, to the NT, WA and all over Australia, carrying their fire-sticks with them to light new fires. This revival fire knew no border or boundary lines as it blazed with the fierce love of the Lord.

My husband Peter and I had the privilege of visiting the site of the Pinnacle Pocket revival. The local Bethel AG Church was led by generations of First Nations Pastors including, Pastor Willie Giblett who operated in a powerful anointing that brought many around him to repentance, including many miracles signs and wonders. In 1959 Pastor Sterling Minniecon was appointed. After that Pastor Eddie Turpin Senior and his wife Aunty Rita who trained up many leaders to take the gospel out to other parts of Australia from the Pinnacle Pocket site of Revival. Pastor Con Spoor was courageously instrumental in this move of God. The revival took place over a few decades in the 1900s and many of our First Nation people and South Sea Islanders were on fire for Jesus. Filled with the Spirit and power of God, they saw manifestation of miracles, signs and wonders as they preached the word of God.

I honour our Christian Elders, leaders and their families who stewarded revival in their time, and I honour those currently leading Churches and communities on the many sites of revival wells.

It is time to get ready for the greatest outbreak of the Holy Spirit and a bursting open of the wells of revival that I believe has already begun. Re-dig the wells, re-dig the wells!
As we stood on the site of the old church we could barely stand up.

I felt like I was in a *power upsurge*, I could see in the Spirit an upward gush of water that erupted from deep in the well and shot up higher than my eyes could see. The powerful anointing that resides there years after the revival is undeniable. These wells of revival over time have been temporarily blocked up and stopped flowing in the same level of power and revival capacity for many and varied reasons. God however, never intended the revival waters to recede.

The good news is, in this new era many of the wells of revival are being re-dug and reopened in the Spirit in a mighty power surge that has not hit earth before. I believe we will see an electric convergence of all these revival wells, in combination with new wells of revival. It will ignite, combust, and converge into one great revival that will sweep the nation and the nations of the earth.

Prayer:

Lord I pray for every hindering boundary line to lift and shift in the name of Jesus. I pray for every divisive spirit to be bound, sent back to the pit of hell, you are now rendered null and void. I pray for the Spirit of reconciliation and unity to be loosed across our land of Australia. I pray for people in

Australia of every tongue, tribe, nation and generation to be reconciled to God and reconciled to one another. I pray for a powerful uniting of every tongue, tribe, nation and generation.

I pray that streams of people join forces as one force to usher in the end time revival, reformation and transformation. I pray for the wells of love to open, the water to surge forth from the wells, shoot up like fountains of revival.

I pray for the ancient wells of revival to burst open, revived with a power surge of heaven that will act as defibrillators to send shock waves through the people to awake them from their slumber. Lord awaken the multitudes to declare the gospel and make Jesus who saves known in the new era. In Jesus name! Amen!

Decree:

I declare and decree that every hindering boundary line to now shift and lift, in Jesus name.

I declare and decree that every divisive spirit at work to divide and conquer is now bound, escorted to the pit of hell and rendered completely null and void, in Jesus name.

I declare and decree that the Spirit of reconciliation love and the Spirit of unity is now loosed across our land of Australia, in immeasurable and accelerated proportions, in Jesus name.

I declare and decree, the blemish of disunity be removed. Now replaced, with Kingdom unity!

I declare and decree Australia, you are now reclaimed by God and reframed for His glory.

I declare and decree that the people in Australia from every tongue, tribe, nation and generation begin to be reconciled to God and to one another, I say come into divine union, in Jesus name.

I declare and decree wells be revived. Wells of revival resurrect. Wells of revival open, with power! Wells of revival surge in the unstoppable power of the Holy Spirit.

I decree ancient wells of revival be released in this nation! In Jesus name! Release the life flow in Jesus name. Amen and Amen!

Footnotes:

(1)   https://aiatsis.gov.au/explore/map-indigenous-australia

(2)   Maps - Gamilaraay/Yuwaalaraay countrydnathan.com

(3)   Location - Kamilaroi - A Nations Identity
        kamilaroianationsidentity.weebly.com

(4)   Location - Kamilaroi - A Nations Identity
        kamilaroianationsidentity.weebly

(5)   Lists 190 & 489 By States – AXYN axyn.com.au

(6)   Official lyric/chord video for "Awake My Soul" by Chris
        Tomlin
        https://www.youtube.com/watch?v=fWpvknKuYrg

(7)   In The River by Jesus Culture ft. Kim Walker-Smith
        https://www.youtube.com/results?search_query=In+the
        +river+Jesus+Culture

(8)   Freedom byJesus Culture - Spotify:
       https://jcltr.lnk.to/livingwithafireY...

(9)   Local Revivals in Australia" by Stuart Piggins
       https://renewaljournal.com/2016/02/28/local-revivals-
       in-australia-bystuart-piggin/

(10)   GOD's FIRE 1-2a Pinnacle Pocket Fire •29 Jun 2012
       John Blackett

(11)   GOD's FIRE 1-3 Innisfail •29 Jun 2012

Chapter 6

A New Sound Rising from the Land

Behold, how good and how pleasant it is for brothers to live together in unity!   2 It is like the precious oil on the head, running down upon the beard, As on Aaron's beard, the oil which ran down upon the edge of his robes. 3 It is like the dew of Hermon Coming down upon the mountains of Zion; For the LORD commanded the blessing there—life forever.

Psalm 133:1-3 NASB

I Love the inclusive heart of the Father for all of His children.

His love has no barriers, no walls, and no borders. It is not a locked-down love, it's a love that knows no bounds, nor division. One love, one people, one family amen!

I believe the church is on the cusp of converging as one, like a mighty army, once dry bones, now *'rattled-up to rise and reign.'*

Family is family where ever you are in the world! Those who are reading this from other Countries, I invite you to come, immerse yourself in this, and let us soak in His love together. Let's eat of His word and drink deeply of His Spirit together. There is no distance in the Spirit. We are Kingdom Family. The Kingdom is within us and the Kingdom spans the universe.

To "drink deeply" of the Spirit is the same as receiving his power and gifts until rivers of living water flow from the inside of us. (See John 3:34; 7:37). Flowing with father's everlasting love!

I want to share with you a part of the Father's heart that I believe He is calling us to gather around right now. The Lord has been revealing this part of His heart to me over the last 18 months or so, through different visions and encounters and the journey He has taken me on through His word. It feels like a supernatural wave that is rising over our nation, and I believe over other nations in this era.

He wants you to know and live in the intimate secret places in His heart. Intimacy is a key that unlocks the mysteries of the heart of the Father. Embrace and absorb revelation of His heart, and wisely steward His heart, along with the things He puts in your heart. The wave is rising over our nation and over your nation. This message is relevant for all nations.

Unity, oneness and family have been in the heart of the Father since before the foundations of the earth. This is a resounding message throughout His word. I believe it is an *ancient key* being released with *fire* to unlock the end time move of God!

I keep hearing both in the Spirit and in the natural

'Diversity in Unity'

The Lord demonstrates diversity and the need we have for one another:

> [17] *Think of it this way. If the whole body were just an eyeball, how could it hear sounds? And if the whole body were just an ear, how could it smell different fragrances?* [18] *But God has carefully designed each member and placed it in the body to function as he desires.* [19] ***A diversity is required***, *for if the body consisted of one single part, there wouldn't be a body at all!* [20] *So now we see that there are many differing parts and functions, but one body.* [21] *It would be wrong for the eye to say to the hand, "I don't need you," and equally wrong if the head said to the foot, "I don't need you."* (1 Corinthians 12:17-21 TPT)

His heart's desire is to see us function as one, and I believe in a John 17:21 *oneness* 'that they may be one (all of us), as we are one (Jesus and the Father). One with Father and one with each other.

Now there is no room for division of any shape or form between Jesus and the Father. They are in perfect unity.

Jesus has infinitely more power to 'unite and ignite' us, as *'one'* unified bride than any devil has to divide and conquer us! In Jesus you are more than a conqueror (see Romans 8:37 NIV).

We are many people groups and we are one Kingdom family! We are many voices and one sound! My sense is that *'mantles are merging and family is forming!'* There is coming a convergence, transference and multiplication of anointing, graces, gifting that will accelerate unity and oneness. This will release the commanded blessing of heaven. I see this will lead to a supernatural explosion and manifestation of the glory of God.

You and I are being invited into this powerful dimension of unity and family oneness! What an overwhelming invitation into the sacred, secret chambers of Father's heart where the ancient seed of family originated. Today it is being birthed through the generations and into the present time. Its life span is eternal. *Unity, oneness and family* is an ancient key to the glorious inheritance for us in this era.

Diversity in unity! I believe *unity* is the *battle strategy of heaven* being released right now. Amen!

I believe that God is setting us up to reap a harvest of the miraculous, and miracles of a magnitude unthinkable! Get ready for an immeasurable outpouring of the supernatural! Are you ready to catch the supernatural wave that is rising?

Generational Prophetic Destinies Called Forth

It's the unity in diverse people groups and the convergence of mantles and divine redemptive gifting's that set us up for the manifestations of the miraculous.

While pondering this, I was taken in the word to Joshua chapter 4 where it tells us about Israel crossing the Jordan:

In verses 4-7 a sublime miracle takes place as the 12 selected men took 12 stones from the middle of the Jordan River and created a memorial with them. Take particular note of verse 7.

> *⁴ Then Joshua called the twelve men whom he had appointed from the children of Israel, one man from every tribe; ⁵ and Joshua said to them: "Cross over before the ark of the LORD your God into the midst of the Jordan, and each one of you take up a stone on his shoulder, according to the number of the tribes of the children of Israel (there are 12 Tribes), ⁶ that this may be a sign among you when your children ask in time to come, saying, 'What do these stones mean to you?' ⁷ Then you shall answer them that the waters of the Jordan were cut off before the ark of the covenant of the LORD; when it crossed over the Jordan, the waters of the Jordan were cut off. And these stones shall be for a memorial to the children of Israel forever."*
> (Joshua 4:4-7 NKJV).

> The TLB version translates verse 7 like this:
> *'You can tell them, 'It is to remind us that the Jordan River stopped flowing when the Ark of God went across!' The monument will be a permanent reminder to the people of Israel of this amazing miracle.'*

Wow, now that is the miraculous power of God. The parting of the Jordan River is an extraordinary demonstration of the power of God that lives on through the generations. I believe there is generational life to the testimony of the building of the monument of remembrance.

These people will be able to testify of God's supernatural miracle working power to the next generation. It is still testifying to us generations later and it will continue to testify to the generations to come.

This passage testifies of the eternal and generational power of God to do supernatural miracles in this day and age and the ages to come. Herein is an ancient key to the new sound rising from the land in this era.

The 12 stones collected from the Jordan River represented twelve diverse tribes. They were one family, and one nation of Israel, yet at the same time, each of the twelve tribes had a different prophetic destiny and were twelve diverse tribes.

While pondering the notion of prophetic destiny, studying and gleaning the prophetic destinies and redemptive gifts and callings highlighted to me from Genesis 49, I received this revelation:

In Genesis 49 before Jacob died he gathered his sons and declared their prophetic destiny over them. This destiny would go on to shape them as tribes generations later.

Let me give you two examples:

Jacob blessed Judah by proclaiming that Judah would "rule over his brothers"; be "like a lion's cub"; and that "the scepter will not depart from Judah" (see Genesis 49:8-10). The scepter speaks of ruling and reigning! King David, and King Solomon were descendants of Judah and Jesus the King of all Kings descended from this tribe. Jesus is "The Lion of the Tribe of Judah (see Revelation 5:5). The scepter did not depart from Judah. Jesus lives and reigns today, generations later through you and I. This is a picture of *generational destiny* being outworked through us today, as the King of glory comes through us (see Psalm 24:7 TPT).

Jacob blessed Issachar whose name means "reward or "recompense" by declaring "when he sees how good is his resting place and how pleasant is his land, he will bend his shoulder to the burden". The land that was allotted to the tribe of Issachar was one of the most fertile land of any of the twelve tribes, and they "saw the land was pleasant" (see Genesis 49:14-15 NIV) and worked it. The sons of Issachar were also famous for 'understanding the times and knowing what Israel should do'. (See 1 Chronicles 12:32).

Over 400 years after Jacob blessed each of his sons and called out their redemptive gifts and callings, we see them being outworked as Israel settles in the land. I believe we are in a time of ancient generational destinies being called forth, in Jesus name!

Each son had a unique calling, which shaped the destiny of their descendants, as they multiplied to become the tribes of Israel. While Israel was one nation, it was made up of twelve distinct tribes. Each with unique redemptive gifts and callings. As they joined together, their gifts and callings complimented each other and contributed to the benefit of the whole nation.

The point here is that there is an ancient old unique prophetic destiny for all tribes. This includes every tongue, tribe, and nation and let me add denomination and generation. This ancient prophetic destiny is being unlocked in us and released through us in this era. For such a time as this! We are all a part of this together!

For instance I believe First Nations People of Australia have a number of redemptive callings, including but not limited to:

- To model community and family (see John 13:34, 35) as we lead people into their true identity and God given authority as sons and daughters of the living God.
- To model family as we gain revelation of living life as brothers and sisters and extended family together in the Kingdom of God.
- Through connection to land and Country, First Nations Christian leaders are called to humbly but assuredly *rise up and lead* this nation in the healing of the land (see 2

Chronicles 7:14). This is beginning to happen through forums like the National Solemn Assembly led by First Nations Apostolic Fathers and Mothers, National Day of Prayer and Fasting, and in other ways too. First Nations Christian Leaders are called to lead this nation in healing the heart of our nation, as the earth groans awaiting the arising of the sons.

- To arise in their redeemed gift of discerning of Spirits for the glory of the Lord.
- To Rise up as First Nations Prophetic Voices of the Land. Many of us grew up experiencing the supernatural realm as natural, knowing and seeing in the Supernatural Spirit realm. This is a redemptive gift and it is for the glory of the one true living God, Jesus Christ our saviour who died on the cross at Calvary for your sin, for my sin, and for the sins of the world. Amen!

These are just a few of the redemptive gifts within the First Nations people groups! There are many more.

All people groups in Australia have redemptive gifts to bring to the Kingdom Family. You have a redemptive gift that the rest of our nation needs. We are all called to enter in to our divine destiny.

Ephesians 4:1-6 TPT

*As a prisoner of the Lord, I plead with you to walk holy, in a way that is suitable to your high rank, given to you in your **divine calling**. [2] With tender humility and quiet patience, always demonstrate gentleness and generous love toward one another, especially toward those who may try your patience.*

*[3] Be faithful to **guard the sweet harmony of the Holy Spirit among you** in the bonds of peace,*

> [4] *being* **one body and one spirit**, *as you were* **all called into the same glorious hope** *of* **divine destiny.** *(Emphasis mine).*

This unity that we are called to function in, isn't unity that comes out of conformity. It's not oneness that comes through uniformity.
It is a unity that flows from a rich diversity and celebration of, and championing of, all cultures, skin colours, and redemptive gifting.

The Sound

Recently, we were driving from Coffs Harbour to Port Macquarie in New South Wales, Australia to join a Kingdom Business Retreat and this happened:

God interrupted and all of a sudden without notice, I was in 'a suddenly moment'. I was taken into an encounter where I had a vision. This is what I saw: I was looking down on a map of Australia, and I saw a First Nations Countryman standing in the land. At the same time I heard the sound of the didgeridoo. I heard a sound rising up through him. It came from deep within the layers of the land of our nation. As the vision went on I heard sounds rising up, the sounds of the didgeridoo, the sounds of the clap sticks, the sounds of the shofar representing Israel, the sound of the Conch shell, and the sound of drums. All resounding as one sound of *wild worship* to the Lord rising up through the land.

There were many sounds, these are the ones that I heard clearly, but I had a knowing that there were many other sounds right there in the Spirit realm, about to break forth. What was about to be released into the atmosphere was a declaration of *oneness.* A declaration of *one family* was being released over our nation.

The Lord is releasing a new sound from this land, this nation of Australia. A mighty army of many instruments and one sound is breaking forth as a glory sound of heaven.

A New Sound Rising from the Land of our Nation!

In this encounter, the Lord then showed me a picture of a *meeting place*, this is the First Nations symbol for where people *gather*. It was made up of dots in a circular formation, each dot in this meeting place was a different colour. The dots were white, shades of brown, (light, medium and dark) black, yellow, and all the ochre colours of the land. These colours represent the diverse skin tones, the diverse people groups living in this land. They were all connected to the sound that was rising up through the land. Right in the middle of the symbol representing the gathering place, there was a cross that spoke loudly. Jesus was at the centre of everything.

On the outside of the gathering place sat symbols representing a man and a woman. There was one at every corner of the nation. In this encounter I knew it represented people of every kind gathering from the four corners of the nation, the north, the south, the east and the west. They were all drawn by the Spirit of God blowing across this nation, all drawn to Jesus as we lift Him up as a banner of love over this nation. The Spirit of God is moving in this land! Amen!

There was not one part of the nation that was untouched. In fact it included all the nations in the Great Southland of the Holy Spirit.

The Lord showed me Torres Strait (part of Queensland Australia), Papua New Guinea, New Zealand and, the South Pacific Islands. They were all part of it. All in it together!

There was a message the Lord was releasing over the land, it was a message that there is one meeting place.
He is calling us to rise up as people gathered together proclaiming the message that in the Father's house there is room for everyone. At the banqueting table there is a seat for you. This message is the sound of *unity,* the sound of *oneness*, the sound of *family*, the *sound of heaven*!

This is the new sound that is rising up from the ancient layers of the land of this nation! It is rising from the hearts of the people in this nation. One heart, one love, one destiny! It sounds like Jesus, it looks like Jesus, and the sweet smelling fragrance it releases smells like Jesus!

One hope, one baptism, one Spirit! One Godhead, the Father, Son and Holy Spirit in perfect unity! Amen!

God has called the church to love and function in unity.

> *Behold, how good and how pleasant it is for brothers to live together in unity!* [2] *It is like the **precious oil** on the head, running down upon the beard, As on Aaron's beard, the oil which ran down upon the edge of his robes.* (Psalm 133:1-2 NASB)

As I write this it feels like glory oil is pouring through my veins and through my whole heart and being. I believe this new dimension of unity will play a part of increasing the knowledge of the glory of the Lord that covers the earth, like the waters cover the sea (see Habakkuk 2:14).

It will be like glory oil pouring through the chambers of many hearts, filling us to overflowing. It will be like glory oil pouring out through the lands of nations and through the waterways to nearby shores. This glory of the Lord will be connecting countries throughout the earth.

> *Verse 3 ^{It} is like the dew of Hermon Coming down upon the mountains of Zion; for the LORD commanded the blessing there—life forever.* (Psalm 133:3 NASB)

The Lord not only blesses unity, He commands a blessing! No devil and no demon is going to stand in the way of the Almighty's command!! Amen! Unity is the battle strategy of heaven and it has the resurrection power of eternal life on it!

As a pre-cursor to this happening I believe there is a call for First Nations people to *'rise and lead'*. To take their place and be part of leading God's people as they themselves are led by the Holy Spirit in these times. I believe this is an *ancient key to the new sound rising from the land in this era.*

I believe this sound of *'one kingdom family'* is like a breaker that will precede a powerful tidal wave of the supernatural that is rising and getting ready to be released. Let's position ourselves to catch and ride this wave?

'Unity, oneness and family' is like a combination code to unlock and break open the end time move of God.

I believe this dimension of unity is a *'fiery ancient key'* to unlock an end time move of God to set the nations ablaze.

Let us be the *'burning ones'* to release it into the earth.

Prayer:

I invite you to agree with me for our nation and your nation at this moment in time? I hear Him again say: *The angels are stationed at their nation.* They are ready to partner with us right now.

Yes for our Nation Australia, but the Lord said '*their*' nation. To me that means the angels are stationed at many nations, including your nation. Whichever nation you are reading this from, I invite you to stand together in prayer and declare over our nation and nations.

Father God we come before your throne of grace, and we stand – united – as one Kingdom family. As the head and not the tail tonight, we trample on the head of the serpent. We stand in our authority against the spirit of division in the powerful name of Jesus. Your word says unity commands a blessing. So Father God we say tear down ancient walls of division in this nation, in the name of Jesus. We say uproot and break ancient old divisive strongholds, and cast them down. Lord, cause the Spirit of Unity to spring up through this land. Lord we come against everything that separates us from you and from one another. We come against everything that divides our hearts and distorts pure love.

Father it is your heart that we are unified, that we love one another, that we cover one another, look out for, protect and stand with one another. Father, your children are standing together as family right now.

Father remove all divisive thoughts and heart attitudes. Forgive us for not forgiving our brothers and sisters the way you have forgiven us.

Forgive us for thinking of ourselves more highly than we should, for making it about us and not you, for not loving our brothers, and our sisters the way you love them Lord.
Create in us a clean heart O Lord and renew a right Spirit within us (see Psalm 51:10-12).

Transform our hearts, renew our minds. As we come together in unity, let us all accelerate from glory to glory and begin to look more like you, smell of your sweet fragrance, and release the sound of heaven.

Lord unite our hearts together this day in the name of Jesus, every colour, every nation, every tribe, every race, every language group, every creed. Every skin tone reflected in the ochre colours of the land and in the gathering place, I decree Lord we are one in you at the table of Family and Oneness. Lord we are one with you and one with each other.

Decree:

WE STAND AS THE BODY OF CHRIST, AND DECREE:

No more division in the name of Jesus, no more separation in the name of Jesus!

We cast the devil out of our mind and out of our hearts in Jesus mighty name!

We decree every hindering way of living, lift and shift off the hearts of the people in our nation!

Every tongue, tribe, people group and nation be reconciled to God and reconciled to one another!

We call you forth as one with God and one with each other.

I say come into divine union in Jesus name!

We decree Kingdom Unity manifest, flow through the arteries of our hearts and the veins of our nation! River of unity – flow!

Unite and ignite us as your warrior bride!

Set us ablaze for you right here, right now Lord!

Fill us with your fire, release your glory!

Release the new sound rising up through us and through this land!

Release the wild worship to the Lord!

We celebrate our uniqueness. We champion diversity. We honour diverse qualities as we unite as one body

We decree the faithfulness to guard the sweet harmony of the Holy Spirit among us in the bonds of peace (see Ephesians 4:1-6 TPT)

We decree we are one body and one Spirit with you. (See Ephesians 4:1-6 TPT)

We decree we are called into the same glorious hope of divine destiny. (See Ephesians 4:1-6 TPT)

We call forth our redemptive gifts for the glory of the living God.

We decree that as we live together in unity it will command blessings of life forever. (See Psalm 133)

We decree 'Kingdom Unity'!!

Shout out Unity! In Jesus Mighty, Mighty Name. Amen and Amen!

Chapter 7

The Angel and the Bride

' that they may all be one; just as You, Father, are in Me and I in You, that they also may be in Us, so that the world may]believe that You sent Me. The glory which You have given Me I also have given to them, so that they may be one, just as We are one; I in them and You in Me, that they may be perfected in unity, so that the world may know that You sent Me, and You loved them, just as You loved Me.' (John 17:21-23 NASB)

..You purchased us to bring us to God - out of every tribe, language, people group, and nation. (Revelations 5:9 TPT)

John 17:21-23 NASB; Revelations 5:9 TPT

Encounter with a Lightning Bolt

As dear friends of ours and highly respected Father and Mother of many nations, Bruce and Cheryl Lindley prayed for me. I suddenly saw a huge glory light heading right for me. I was completely consumed by this light. In that instant lightning broke out all around me in the Spirit realm. In a split second a lightning bolt struck me in the spirit. It pierced right through me, and penetrated deep into the earth, deep within the layers of the land. In an instant I was awakened to ancient old strongholds being *struck down* and in the same split second *new song-lines* of *wild worship* to the Lord were being *established* in this land.

A voice boomed: 'The Lord's power has struck!!'

Psalm 29:7 NIV tells us:
The voice of the Lord strikes with flashes of lightning.

That is how it felt, like flashes of lightning striking with a message from the Lord. The sense was that time itself, time before the foundations of the earth; along with time from a place in the heavenly realms; and time at that very moment – collided and all synced in one split moment. In that very moment in time it was as if heaven had released onto the earth a great surge of power and authority the land has not encountered before. In that same instant, it was like the ancient realms came forth and were propelled into eternity. This explosive transaction that took place seemed to cross all timelines, ages, realms and dimensions.

The ancient wisdom of Christian ancestors who are now part of the great cloud of witnesses were drawing forth the ancient wisdom of heaven, making it available to us in this generation.

They were making withdrawals from the *'tears and prayers of intercession (TPI)'* like an Automatic Transaction Machine (ATM) where these prayers had been deposited into the plan for our divine destiny on our behalf. I believe we will see a great return on those *'tears and prayers of intercession (TPI)'* in this new era. I believe the return will be in the form of a *'harvest of the miraculous'* from the seeds that were sown in prayer and intercession from another timeline by our ancestors and forefathers.

Throughout this decade and this new era I believe we can expect to see a *'harvest of the miraculous in lightning bolt - wild power of God'*.

There will be encounters with Jesus that will stop people in their tracks and leave them *love struck* and in *awe* of the *one true living God*.

From that moment of prayer with Bruce and Cheryl, for the following five days and nights straight, we experienced lightning bolts and thunder in the natural realm.

As I was driving home in an electrical storm, there were lightning bolts in the natural realm shooting vertically, straight down into the land. I felt it was a declaration of the Lord, announcing that there was a series of *'mighty power surges'* about to break forth into the land, throughout our nation and the nations. It will come through us as His awe struck conduits.

I believe that this decade and this new era will be pregnant with, and birth electrical blueprints from heaven.
'A John 14 greater works power surge' is being released into and through the sons and daughters of King Jesus.

"I tell you this **timeless truth**: The person who follows me in faith, believing in me, will do the same mighty miracles that I do—**even greater miracles** than these because I go to be with my Father! For I will do whatever you ask me to do when you **ask me in my name**. And that is how the Son will show what the Father is really like and bring glory to him. (John 14:12, 13 TPT)

The astonishing miracles and countless wonders performed by Jesus during His earthly ministry were nothing short of stunning. Jesus changed the lives of everyone around Him everywhere He went. John 21:25 sums up the magnitude of His impact "Jesus did many other things as well. If every one of them was written down, I suppose that even the whole world would not have room for the books that would be written." Yet we have been gifted provision for the astonishing John 14:12 promise to do greater works than He. As I studied the miracles Jesus performed I found this promise mind blowing!

Now I am going to share just a few of the miracles Jesus did to give us some perspective on what this new era holds for us. Now I'm not saying that it will be all rosy, we are aware that the days will get darker as darkness covers the earth in the end times (see Isaiah 60:2), but we also know and stand on the truth that as the days get darker, the glory increases and the light shines brighter through us (see Isaiah 60:1, 3).

A snapshot of some of Jesus miracles starts at Cana of Galilee at the wedding where Jesus did the first of the signs through which He revealed His glory as he turned the water into wine (John 2:1-11). Through this miracle His newly formed band of disciples believed Him. Jesus healed the royal official's son who was in His sickbed close to death in Capernaum (John 4:46-47).

Jesus told Peter to cast their net on the other side of the boat, after a long and unsuccessful night of fishing. When they did they brought in a great haul of fish. Having witnessed such an extraordinary miracle they left everything and followed Jesus (Luke 5:1-11). Jesus cast out an unclean spirit and news about him spread quickly over the whole region of Galilee (Mark 1:23-28); Jesus healed Peter's mother-in-law of a fever, the fever left and she began to wait on them (Mark 1:30-31). He healed a leper and people came from everywhere to hear Him (Mark 1:40-45). He cleansed 10 lepers (Luke 17:11-19). Jesus raised the widow's dead son and the large crowd and His disciples were all filled with awe and praised God (Luke 7:11-18). Jesus delivered two demoniacs (Matthew 8:28-34). He healed the paralytic and when the crowd saw this, they were filled with awe; and they praised God, who had given such authority to man (Matthew 9:1-8). Jesus healed the woman with the issue of blood as she pushed through the crowd to touch the hem of Jesus garment and her faith healed her, then she went in peace (Luke 8:43-48). Jesus opened blind eyes (Matthew 9:27-31). Jesus drove out a demon and a man who was mute spoke, Jesus loosed his tongue, and the crowd was amazed and said 'nothing like this has ever been seen in Israel' (Matthew 9:32-33). He opened deaf ears by simply saying "Ephphatha" which means "Be opened!", the man's ears were opened, his tongue was loosened and he began to speak plainly (Mark 7:31-37). He raised Lazarus from the dead (John 11:1-46). These are just a few of the miracles our Saviour did during His earthly ministry.

Could I encourage us to truly brace ourselves with fortified faith, trust and belief in God's word that as we follow Jesus in faith, surrendered to Him, believing in Him, we will do the same mighty miracles that Jesus did and **even greater miracles** than these because Jesus went to be with the Father!

Jesus is now seated at the right hand of the Father and anything we ask in His name, He will do. This is how Jesus will show what the Father is really like and bring glory to him. All glory is yours Father.

We are about to step into the greatest days of walking with increased authority and lightning bolt power and even greater miracles that the Lord is entrusting to His sons and daughters in this hour.

How much more do you want to fall on your knees before Him and give Him glory? Your deep and genuine surrender to Jesus will be instrumental to catapult you into the very sacred place in the Spirit realm. Entry into this place, will *'flick the switch'* that ignites the *power surge* that will release the *power of God* through us, in the *'even greater'* measure. We will be the conduit for this power surge to be released into the nation. I see the power will travel through the remnant and shoot out into the nations. It will be like lightning striking the ground and travelling through the land.

I feel a strong urge right here to encourage us to lean into James 4:8. Draw near to God and watch how he draws near to you. Feel the gentle guidance and purposeful pull to lean into Jesus and let Him guide you into the deep secret place of uninterrupted intimacy with Him alone. He is the power source, the ultimate source of all power. It is Him we want to release into the world around us, Jesus.

In this encounter that I was describing, I heard the word *'volition.'* Now I admit that I needed to get a better understanding of what volition meant.

So I looked it up. It means this:

Webster Definition: Volition

'The power of choosing or determining; an act of making a choice or decision; choice or decision made.' Synonyms include *free will.*

Clearly the Lord was alerting me to a warning out of Joshua 24:15 to choose this day whom you will serve.

> 'But if serving the LORD seems undesirable to you, then choose this day for yourselves whom you will serve, whether the gods your ancestors served beyond the Euphrates, or the gods of the Amorites, in whose land you are living. But as for me and my household, we will serve the LORD.' (Joshua 24:15 NIV)

The scripture either side of James 4:8 and the remainder of verse 8 was magnified on the screen of my mind.

> [7-10] So let God work his will in you. Yell a loud *no* to the Devil and watch him make himself scarce. Say a quiet *yes* to God and he'll be there in no time. Quit dabbling in sin. Purify your inner life. Quit playing the field. Hit bottom, and cry your eyes out. The fun and games are over. Get serious, really serious. Get down on your knees before the Master; it's the only way you'll get on your feet. (James 4:7-10 MSG)

If it is not already settled firmly in your spirit, let me encourage you to *make the choice* without wavering. Here is the warning: If you choose the enemy and the ways of the world, there will be no power surge of lightning bolt power of God from heaven. Be warned the potential for a power surge from darkness is as real as the power surge from heaven. The enemy counterfeits what God is doing to try to trick us. Choosing darkness reaps a whirlwind of darkness and evil.

Choosing Jesus reaps a whirlwind of the goodness of God, and the greater glory works and the divine power surge that glorifies Jesus. Our decisions determine our destiny. Our decisions today hold the consequences of our tomorrows.

Just as the seed of prayer and intercession to Jesus positions us to command the land to yield a harvest for the Kingdom of God, and our surrendered hearts and lives to the Lord positions us to *flick the switch* to the *power surge of heaven* – so too, the sin and darkness sown by demonic occult and witchcraft activity along with other *sin seed* sown by the enemy – will manifest in your life and in your world.

I am reminded of John 10:10 right here:

> The thief does not come except to steal, and to kill, and to destroy. I have come that they may have life, and that they may have it more abundantly. (John 10:10 NKJV).

The Lord would say: 'choose this day who you will serve'. I would like to add this challenge, to choose this day *how* you will serve and *how much* of your life is laid down to serve our King Jesus.

Your humility and consecration to the Lord will attract the power surge of the lightning bolt power of God, along with manifestations of the miraculous in the form of greater works than He.

The Angel

During this time of encounter I was caught up in the Spirit above the electrical storm. Right before me was a huge angel. I knew it was a National angel. It was so magnificent! I was in awe of God our creator and the works of His hands. The *colours* in its wings struck me.

There were white, cream, ivory, shades of light, medium, dark browns, black, reddish, yellow and even orange tinge tones.

I saw a glory light move through the angel's wings. Each colour was highlighted and shimmered with life. It seemed to me like resurrection life that was full of power and joy. Each feather in the wings was lined and overlayed with gold. Magnificent! It was as if the Lord was about to make an announcement and present something of great value.

Every feather moved upward in unison. The sound was the sound of *a radiant bride arising as one*! Triumphant and joyous, trumpets resounded through the airways, travelled through the land-ways and even under the waterways. This sound seemed to travel out to the shores and lands of the surrounding Islands of the South Pacific!

This particular angel was displaying the splendour of the Lord. It carried the sound of one accord.

The Bible teaches us that angels exist as created spirit beings, created to worship and serve God. They are a company created to minister to the heirs of salvation.

> [14] Are not the angels all ministering spirits (servants) sent out in the service [of God for the assistance] of those who are to inherit salvation? (Hebrews 1:14 AMPC)

> [17] and if children, then heirs—heirs of God and joint heirs with Christ (Romans 8:17 NKJV)

We do not worship angels we worship Jesus. Jesus, LORD of all, spoke of the angels often and He himself was ministered to by them (Mark 8:38; 13:32; Matthew 13:41; John 1:51; 2 Thessalonians 1:7; Hebrews 12:22). That said angels are mentioned in the Bible 273 times. A few of these include:

Revelations 14: 6 NIV
Then I saw another angel flying in mid heaven, and he had the eternal gospel to proclaim to those who live on the earth—to every nation, tribe, language and people.

Psalm 103: 20 NIV
Praise the LORD, you his angels, you mighty ones who do his bidding, who obey his word.

John 1:50-51
50 Jesus said, "You believe because I told you I saw you under the fig tree. You will see greater things than that." 51 He then added, "Very truly I tell you, youᴶ will see 'heaven open, and the angels of God ascending and descending on' the Son of Man."

Many encounters with an angel are mentioned in the bible, for example:

Angels Come to John in Prison:
It's difficult to read the Book of Revelation without running into an angel. From the mention of angels in seven churches (Revelation 1-3) to the angels blaring the seven trumpets (Revelation 8) these heavenly beings permeate the pages of the last book in the New Testament.

But these visions and angels came to John at an interesting time. As an old man, imprisoned on the island of Patmos, he had seen countless brothers and sisters in Christ endure persecution and martyrdom at the hands of the Romans. In fact, of the twelve disciples, he alone had evaded martyrdom when he wrote Revelation.

Furthermore, John witnessed the destruction of the temple in 70 A.D., or at least, must have caught word about it. He needed a message of hope in difficult times.

He received it through his encounters with the angels and the visions he marked down in Revelation.

(1) Source:https://bible.knowing-jesus.com/topics/Angels,-Ot-Appearances

Daniel 10:13 Gabriel coming to overthrow the prince of Persia: But the prince of Persia opposed me for 21 days. Then Michael came to help me. He is one of the leaders of the angels. He helped me win the battle over the king of Persia. (NIRV)

The Bride

As the encounter continued, right before my eyes and in mid-air this magnificent angel morphed into a mature, and radiant bride. The angels' feathers *now formed the bridal dress* adorned and displayed by the bride. The colours that appeared on the angel's wings were now the same coloured feathers that made up this most stunning bridal dress.

From high up in the encounter my attention moved from the angel to the land of Australia. As I looked down onto the continent of Australia, it was like my eyes were sharpened in the Spirit as my vision zoomed in and became like x-ray vision peering into the layers of the land. The Lord showed me the many colours of the land in our nation. These colours were the ochre colours embedded in the land, even to the orange and yellow colours in the Tasmanian landscape by the sea.

The colours in the *angels' wings*, the *Brides Dress*, and the *ochre colours of the land* were pertinent to the announcement and presentation being made by the Lord of Hosts. Each colour - represented the *diverse skin tones* of the many people groups in our nation – Australia!

..You purchased us to bring us to God - out of every tribe, language, people group, and nation. (Revelations 5:9 TPT)

I knew in that instant that the Lord was announcing the magnificent facets of his Australian Bride in a regal, extravagant, elaborate, glorious and splendid way. To Australia and to the nations of the world, it was as if He was revealing His *'Bride of many nations within this nation'*.

This encounter was surrounded with the sense like Debutantes being presented to family and loved ones at a Debutante Ball. It signifies coming of age, a modern day rite of passage into maturity being presented to community.

When I think of a debutante ball I am reminded of what it means for my family and some of our communities. The young lady is being presented to loved ones and the world in a sense as a magnificent, treasured, and beautiful precious gift. Usually she is partnered by a male relative from community who valiantly protects and partners with her with the purpose to enhance her shine.

This is the sense in this encounter that Father God is about to present His exquisite Australian Bride in all her unique glory. This signifies that she is coming into great maturity. All the while, Father is guarding and guiding His Australian bride into her full destiny.

I believe God is forging a fortified and glorious bride. As the different people groups and cultures *converge* into *one kingdom culture,* secure in their true identity as the sons and daughters of the King of Kings, we have a Bride emerging, who displays His glory and splendour. There is a strong sense of mantles merging and a new oneness emerging. This bride signifies that the Body of Christ in Australia is entering a new level of maturity. The Song of Solomon is a beautiful picture of the maturing bride being courted by the King. She starts off feeling ugly 'I am darkened by the sun' (1:6), 'my own vineyard I have neglected' (1:6) and immature 'her breasts are not yet grown' (8:8),

She emerges a radiant bride, 'who is this that appears like the dawn, fair as the moon, bright as the sun, majestic as the stars in procession' (6:10). The King describes her as 'beautiful as Tirzah, as lovely as Jerusalem, as majestic as troops with banners, turn your eyes from me, they overwhelm me' (6:4, 5). 'My breasts are like towers' (8:10) (a sign of maturity and a sign of a woman able to nurture and feed others). This bride, having encountered various trials and painful separations from the King emerges a mature radiant and beautiful bride fit for her bridegroom king.

In the vision of the angel and the bride, a huge golden ring appeared and came into focus. The gold was a deep, rich colour. This ring spoke clearly of His Australian Bride in all its diverse cultures, nationalities and denominations entering into covenant relationship with each other and with Him.

The first time we hear of covenant in the Scriptures is in Genesis 17 where God appeared to Abraham and said, 'I am God Almighty' (v 1), 'I will make an everlasting covenant between me and you and your descendants after you for the generations to come, to be your God and the God of your descendants after you' (v 7).

In this vision of the gold ring God was speaking of the body of Christ in Australia coming together in covenant oneness as a unified bride made ready for the Bridegroom
There is an invitation! I believe we are being invited into a higher dimension of unity, a John 17:21-23 oneness. Jesus described this unity and oneness when he prayed,

'that they may all be one; just as You, Father, are in Me and I in You, that they also may be in Us, so that the world may [1]believe that You sent Me. The glory which You have given Me I also have given to them, so that they may be one, just as We are one; I in them and You in Me, that they may be perfected in unity, so that the world may know that You sent Me, and You loved them, just as You loved Me.' (John 17:21-23)

The strategy: Unity is a battle strategy of heaven being released! I heard the Lord say:

'My angel armies are stationed at their nation ready to run and war.

That is with the decrees coming from a *unified bride*.

The Bible tells us that the angels are on assignment to partner with us as the heirs of salvation to execute the word and plans of the Lord (see Hebrews 1:14).
The Lord is inviting us to co-govern the affairs of the earth in divine partnership with Him and His angels through Spirit-led divine revelation, strategies and blueprints from heaven.

The angelic hosts are stationed at nations ready to run and war with us, to 'protect, defend, and guard us in all our ways of obedience and service (see Psalm 91:11). They receive their orders from the Commander of the Lord of hosts and are dispatched from the throne room of heaven, move throughout the nations in the earth at the declaration of His word to see the word of God accomplished.

May He equip and empower us all to become the mature and unified Bride who sees what He is doing in the realms of the Spirit, who hears what the Spirit is saying, and who executes the blueprints of heaven to see His Kingdom come and His will be done in all its glorious fullness to the very ends of the Earth throughout this new era.

There is a purpose! This *unity and oneness* marks His mature *remnant army of reformers* rising in this land to overthrow and overturn royal thrones and shatter the power of foreign kingdoms (see Haggai 2:22). They are seated at the right hand of the Father ready to co-rule and reign with Christ to see the will of God established in the earth.

Let me talk about unity as a battle strategy. There have been demonic strongholds over cities, regions, states, the nation, and people groups that will only be broken and destroyed when the body of Christ comes together in unity and uses its authority to break these stronghold and release those being oppressed by the enemy.

When Jesus said 'I will build my church and the gates of hell will not prevail against it' (Matthew 16:18) He used the word 'ekklesia' translated 'church.'

He could have said I will build my synagogue or my temple, but instead he used a secular term that was commonly understood and used by the Greeks and Romans. It was a term that referred to an assembly of people 'called out' of the population to govern the affairs of a city or nation – in essence, it was a city council, parliament or congress.

To the Romans, it was a group of people sent into a conquered region to rule it, but also to alter the culture until it became like Rome, realizing this was the ideal way to control their empire.

They changed government, social structure, language, schools, etc., until the people talked, thought, acted like, and considered themselves Romans.

The church is starting to arise and realise they have been commissioned to disciple nations. The church has been called to rule and reign with Christ, seated with Him in the heavenly realms, equipped with the keys of the Kingdom of God to loose and bind. They are the 'ekklesia,' the governing assembly called to bring transformation to the nations. As they arise as one in unity, I believe they will be better equipped to fulfil their commission to disciple nations.

What does it mean for Australia?

As I was coming into the New Year 2021 in the new decade and new era, I saw in the Spirit '2021' written vertically. The numbers 2 and 1 came swiftly into focus as a countdown, and I heard

3-2-1- Blast off!

I believe as we converge as God's people, representing every tongue, tribe, nation denomination and generation, the Lord is launching us, the Australian Bride, into a new dimension in the Spirit realm through a portal, a door of *ancient wisdom and revelation'*. As this happens the *switch is flicked* and *lightning bolt power will strike* Australia and the nations.

I see Australia will be launched as a spearhead to pierce through the enemy's divisive film over many lands. To lead and help bring unity and oneness as we model this in our own land. This spearhead of unity and oneness will break open the realms of the lightning bolt power of the miraculous waiting to manifest through the people of the lands. This spearhead was highlighted and emphasized to me.

Spearhead

Definition: spearhead
The spearhead of a campaign is the person or group that leads it. Spearhead a movement.

I believe this to be true of the Australian Bride. She will arise as a new breed of unity and oneness to lead this movement in partnership with Holy Spirit across the lands.

Spearhead:
1. The pointed head of a spear; the leading force in a military attack
2. Any person or thing that leads or initiates an attack
3. To take the lead

Synonyms: 'lead, head, pioneer, launch, set off, initiate, lead the way, set in motion, and blaze the trail.'

I decree: 'Australia, you are a trail blazer!'

Synonyms Hebrew: Military unit, military force, military group

I believe from Australia is rising a remnant army of reformers from each people group, arising together, in one accord to lead the way. It is a remnant army of special-forces, highly trained and ready for battle. Ready to take the land, emerging as a triumphant victor equipped to tear down strongholds and foreign kingdoms and to build up the Kingdom of God across the lands.

When I think of a spearhead, I think of stone and flint, and then fire. As we keep our eyes firmly fixed like flint on Jesus, and Him as the living word, and as we dwell in His presence, this is what activates and ignites the fire within us and the fire that will blaze a trail across the land.

It is this flint-like focus that enables us to hit the target with the word of God that never comes back void and accomplish all it is set out to accomplish (see Isaiah 55:11. It is this flint like focus that empowers us to spearhead the nations as an army and break open the way to enter into the ancient realms of wisdom and revelation.

As cultures converge within the Australian Bride, she will be launched like a rocket to spearhead the ancient realms of wisdom and revelation, to then impart new dimensions of power and authority to the nations in this new era.

Australia arise in maturity and all authority, united as one!

Footnotes:

(1) Source:https://bible.knowing-jesus.com/topics/Angels,-Ot-Appearances

John 1:51 (AMP)
Then He said to him, "I assure you *and* most solemnly say to you, you will see heaven opened and the angels of God ascending and descending on the Son of Man [the bridge between heaven and earth]."

Psalm 91:11-12 (AMP):
[11] For He will command His angels in regard to you, to protect *and* defend *and* guard you in all your ways [of obedience and service]. [12] They will lift you up in their hands, So that you do not [even] strike your foot against a stone.

Matthew 16: 27 (NIVUK)
For the Son of Man is going to come in his Father's glory with his angels, and then he will reward each person according to what they have done.

Chapter 8

Australia You Are My Burning One!

For our God is a consuming fire (Hebrews 12:29 NKJV)

20 Now to him who is able to do immeasurably more than all we ask or imagine, according to his power that is at work within us, 21 to him be glory in the church and in Christ Jesus throughout all generations, for ever and ever! Amen. (Ephesians 3:20 NIV).

(Hebrews 12:29 NKJV; Ephesians 3:20 NIV)

While travelling in the car and praying for Australia, I kept hearing sirens. When I looked around me I could not see any sign of a State Emergency Service (SES) vehicle. It was then that I knew the Lord was speaking to me through my spiritual Senses.

Vision: 🔥 As I looked into the sky, through an open eye vision, I saw a flame. Immediately, in the Spirit, the airways were set ablaze with fiery flames. The skyline combusted and was engulfed in fire.

I heard the Lord say:

'HOLY FIRE'

My Spirit instantly knew that the purpose of this holy fire was to burn up the old and what is not holy, to make room for the new *'wholly filling of Holy fire.'* The kind of fire that leads you through the eye of a needle, for you to then come out into a wide open space of freedom.

As the airways across Australia burned, I sensed that the demonic strongholds that had governed the airways were being destroyed.

I heard the Lord say:

'My HOLY FIRE is hovering over My Beloved'

I felt the Lords intense love and fierce protection for His beloved Australian bride?

Then I heard the Lord say:

'My flaming fire marks this territory as my own. Australia you are mine!'

Right then in my vision, I saw the Lion of the Tribe of Judah, pounce on the continent of Australia and fiercely *ROAR*. The breath of God is being released upon you Australia, to reclaim you to the Kingdom of God. He is roaring over the timeline of this country, and setting the coastlines ablaze.

I saw in the Spirit, the hand of the Lord and in it were flames. As He opened his hand, I could see He was sending the flames of fire down into Australia. They were like arrows with coordinates that had been pre-set to locate, strike and ignite its target with pinpoint precision.

I believe the Lord is saying, I will strategically drop My flame into those who carry my heart and my pre-destined eternal flame to reign. That is, those who are already on fire for God, secure in their identity as co-rulers, reigning with Christ. They will be those who are postured, ready to catch and release. I see it instantly igniting a blazing passion within those hungry to apprehend and release this fiery LOVE throughout the nation.

Jesus in His glory in heaven is clothed in fire and surrounded by fire. His eyes are like blazing fire (Revelation 1:14 NIV).

His feet are like bronze glowing in a furnace (see Revelation 1:15 NIV), and His face is like the sun shining in all its brilliance (see Revelation 1:16 NIV). Holy Spirit before the throne is described as 'seven lamps blazing, these are the seven Spirits of God' (Revelation 4:5 NIV). Before the throne is a sea of glass mixed with fire (Revelation 15:2 NASB).

Fire features heavily in John's description of heaven. Fire speaks of purity and passion.

When the Lord addresses the seven churches in the Book of Revelation, he says to the church as Laodicea, 'you are neither cold nor hot; I wish that you were cold or hot. [16] So because you are lukewarm, and neither hot nor cold, I will vomit you out of My mouth. [17] Because you say, "I am rich, and have become wealthy, and have no need of anything," and you do not know that you are wretched, miserable, poor, blind, and naked, [18] I advise you to buy from Me gold refined by fire so that you may become rich, ... (Revelation 3:16-18 NASB).

He was calling them to repent of their complacency and invest in the eternal things that are 'refined gold' so that they can be truly rich.

Gold in this verse refers to those things that have eternal value.

Paul wrote [12] Now if anyone builds on the foundation with gold, silver, precious stones, wood, hay, or straw, [13] each one's work will become evident; for the day will show it because it is to be revealed with fire, and the fire itself will test [a]the quality of each one's work. [14] If anyone's work which he has built on it remains, he will receive a reward. [15] If anyone's work is burned up, he will suffer loss; but he himself will be saved, yet only so as through fire. (1 Corinthians 3:12-15 NASB).

Our works on earth will be tested by fire. If the works are consumed by fire we will suffer loss. However if we let the fire of God purge us now, our works will be built on a foundation of 'gold', silver and precious stones and we will receive an eternal reward accordingly.

As we allow the fire of God to purge and refine us we will manifest more and more of His life, power and glory.

Saints in the past like Smith Wigglesworth carried such an anointing and fire that without a word being spoken, those that came into His proximity were convicted of sin and began to cry out to God in repentance. We read in Acts 5 where those that came into Peter's proximity as he passed by were healed of their sicknesses (verse 15). We know that those who touched the hem of Jesus' garment pulled power out of Him to be healed (Mark 5:27-30).

I believe we are coming into the days where those who are willing to allow the Lord to burn away sin and ignite them with fire will manifest miracles and convict people of sin without a word being spoken.

This flame that I saw the Lord drop into those who carry His heart, was like a supernatural proximity sensor. As the ones who carried this charged flame came into close proximity with another person afflicted by the enemy, the flame reacted like a proximity sensor. It detected the things that need to be sanctified and made holy within the individual. This sensor flame had a dual effect. First it purged and cleansed, causing people to repent of their sin. Then it ignited the greater dimensions of miracles signs and wonders available to us, so those who received this were empowered to walk in a greater measure of Isaiah 61:1-3 anointing. This sensor flame is an anointing.

The Spirit of the Sovereign LORD is on me, because the LORD has anointed me to proclaim good news to the poor. He has sent me to bind up the broken-hearted, to proclaim freedom for the captives and release from darkness for the prisoners, ² to proclaim the year of the LORD's favour and the day of vengeance of our God, to comfort all who mourn, ³ and provide for those who grieve in Zion— to bestow on them a crown of beauty instead of ashes, the oil of joy instead of mourning, and a garment of praise instead of a spirit of despair. They will be called oaks of righteousness, a planting of the LORD for the display of his splendour. (Isaiah 61:1-3 NIV)

Those set ablaze with this flame will enter into a *John 14:12 greater works*, and launch from the shoulders of **Matthew 10:8** *heal the sick, raise the dead, and cleanse the lepers, cast out demons.*

The hearts of those being supernaturally purged, cleansed and empowered are handled with extreme care, a pure heart and the Father's love. This draws his sons and daughters to Himself. It is always honouring and never intended to embarrass, hurt or shame. This impartation carries the heart of our loving Father. As you get closer, the anointing carried in the flame begins to eradicate that which is foreign to the Kingdom of God. Hindrances that would stop the person from entering into pure intimacy with the Lord and from receiving their full inheritance begin to burn up.

Therefore, rid yourselves of all malice and all deceit, hypocrisy, envy, and slander of every kind. ² Like newborn babies, crave pure spiritual milk, so that by it you may grow up in your salvation, ³ now that you have tasted that the Lord is good.

(1 Peter 2:1-3 NIV)
So abandon every form of evil, deceit, hypocrisy, feelings of jealousy and slander. [2] In the same way that nursing infants cry for milk, you must intensely crave the pure spiritual milk *of God's Word*. For this "milk" will cause you to grow into maturity, fully nourished and strong for life — [3] especially now that you have had a taste of the goodness of Yahweh and have experienced his kindness. (1 Peter 2:1-3 TPT)

As we are exposed to this burning up, we are transformed from the inside out.

Fire to Transform a Nation:

I hear the Lord say:

'Watch and see Me spread throughout the landscape, transforming and re-forming this nation.'

Not by might, not by power but by my Spirit says the Lord of hosts.' (Zechariah 4:6 NIV).

The breath of God is released, the flame travels through the landscape, consuming the hearts of the people, and transforming the heart of the nation. I sense a fullness in the Lord's heart. He knows there are many *'ready ones'* on the ground and He has pinpoint precision. Are you ready to catch this flaming impartation to take it and release it into the sphere of influence you have been given?

The Lord said to me:

'There are areas of your life that have been ruled by the enemy up to now, and the Lord would say 'no more. I am blazing a trail through the chambers of your heart, through the fibres of your being. I am setting a fire in your bones, for I am a consuming fire' (see   Hebrews 12:29)

I believe He then said:

'I am setting ablaze within you an eternal flame. You will become My eternal torch. My breath will ignite a flame in you for eternal reign'

This speaks to me of the everlasting love of the Lord that burns eternally within us. His love shines through us. Holy Spirit within us reigns eternal.

Then I heard the Lord say:

'With precision ignition I am setting ablaze within you an eternal fiery flame. I am igniting a wildfire that will spread across the spiritual airways, land, and water ways'

Not too long ago, we saw fire devastate our Australian landscape in the natural realm. I believe the fires, as devastating as they were, are a prophetic sign in the natural realm that points to what God wants to do spiritually throughout Australia.

> *The spiritual did not come first, but the natural, and after that the spiritual* (1 Corinthians 15:46 NIV).

Even though the natural fires caused much heart ache and devastation for many, the fire of God coming upon us is not the slightest bit destructive or sent to harm us in anyway. It is quite the opposite! it reflects the tender loving kindness of the Father's heart. He turns all that was meant for evil, around for good, for those who love Him.

I sense the Lord saying:

'Watch now how My eternal spiritual fire will supernaturally set ablaze a sunburned country for the bounty of My sonship, My Kingdom bounty.

The sense I had was that the great Southland of the Holy Spirit which many of our intercessors, you and I included, have all sown into through prayer over many years, will reap a harvest of *'Kingdom transformers and reformers'* like none before. Sons and daughters will be baptised in Sonship and raised up to know their authority in this era.

Burning To Birth

I heard the Lord say this:

'I am burning away the old – the old mindsets, old wine skin, old ways of leading, governing, trading and aligning. I am **burning to birth my original purpose,** in more of its fullness. **Fire to burn up, and fire to bring forth**. I am **back-burning** to the time of your birth, **to bring you forth** in all My glory, My New Era-Glory. I am back-burning through the historic generational line, to rid you of age old cursing, to then bring you forth in generational blessing and to fill you with new era wine. I am back-burning to birth a fresh new move of My burning ones'

Australia You Are My Burning One

Then I heard the Lord say this:

'I am setting before you *a holy fire* 🔥 preparing you my bride. Cleansing, purging, re-constructing, and re-moving, to *re-create and impregnate* my burning ones with My Kingdom blueprints, plans and purposes to be birthed into this land, in these times. It will be fire to burn up, and fire to bring forth.

This fire will be like an end time fire, an eternal flame that will not be snuffed out. It has now begun. **Australia, you are my burning one.'**

I believe the Lord is releasing fire to burn up, and fire to bring forth the gold, and the harvest in our nation. The breath of God will blow over the land to see this fire spread. It will ignite those of every tongue, tribe and generation in the nation. They will be ignited with a flame that burns eternally causing them to rise up to rule and reign, as Kingdom heirs in this new era. They will be secure in their true identity as the Sons and Daughters of the King.

Get ready to enter new dimensions, and be set ablaze in new ways. Get ready to be transformed and go out into all the nation. To release the Kingdom blueprints, plans and purposes you carry. This could be the dreams you have had in your heart, the visions, the encounters and revelations you've had from time spent in the sacred secret place with Jesus.

My encouragement to us all is to let the Lord do his refining work in you to burn up the stuff that hinders you.
To burn up the stuff that stops you from stepping into your destiny, or stops you having the confidence to be bold and courageous as you go forth armed with the gospel. He is about to *birth and reap* a harvest of Kingdom transformers and reformers like none before.

Fireballs from Heaven Hurled into His Burning Ones

I entered a fiery encounter with the Lord where I saw fire balls shoot like lightning strikes, down into the land of this nation. These balls of fire from heaven, were launched into the land of this nation with a Joshua 1:6, 7, 9 and 18 purpose to be very bold and courageous.

[6] Be strong and courageous, because you will lead these people to inherit the land I swore to their ancestors to give them.

[7] "Be strong and very courageous. Be careful to obey all the law my servant Moses gave you; do not turn from it to the right or to the left, that you may be successful wherever you go.

[9] Have I not commanded you? Be strong and courageous. Do not be afraid; do not be discouraged, for the LORD your God will be with you wherever you go."

[18] Whoever rebels against your word and does not obey it, whatever you may command them, will be put to death. Only be strong and courageous!" (Joshua 1:6, 7, 9, 18 NIV)

I saw these balls of fire strike the land. As they did, flames shot out in many directions, mirroring the spread of lightning across the skyways.

These bolts of lightning travelled through the ancient veins of the land like lightning. This fireball of boldness travelled at speed across the land and carried the power of God, in volumes greater than has been seen or felt to date. The rumbling of ancient sounds converged from the ages to explode into the now. I sensed that the momentum is growing at lightning speed, the force of the power source is beyond our imagination. It spreads across vast spans of land mass. As it moved, the Spirit of God was moving with it across this nation. The Spirit of God pinpointed and struck its target.

Boldness and courage was fiercely imparted into the target. This impartation contains an ancient warrior valour, along with gallantry, bravery and boldness.

It is intended to manifest in the rising of the warrior Spirit and displays of gallantry. This equipping of supernatural boldness will be needed for the days of battle ahead of us in this new era. Enemy territory will be taken. Sniper like assignments will be executed. The fireballs of boldness will be seen in the warriors arising to take this land for Jesus. Amen.

Their fireballs of boldness have written on them "family" "unity" "oneness" "apostles, prophets, pastors, evangelists, teachers" "watchman" "gate-keepers" "intercessors" "Tiddas' and some with 'voices of the land' written on them. These are only some of the many targets in these times. These are targets of an ageless timeline of heaven. Ordained before the foundations of the earth, these are ancient keys to the new era.

Camp-Fire Encounter with Jesus

I was in my lounge room sitting on the floor in God's presence, just worshipping Jesus. I looked and in the Spirit I saw two feet, legs and the hem of a robe. Could it be? Glory filled the house. I gasped and looked up. It was Jesus! I was at the feet of Jesus right there in in my lounge room, in total awe of His holiness, incandescence, magnificence and regal majesty. Jesus leaned down to me, he held my face in his hands. In that moment, an intense kabod glory fell on me! The whole world dissipated before me, and I was completely consumed with Jesus. He began to blow on me, blowing the breath of God in to me.

Instantaneously I became illuminated kindling in his hands. He blew on me and full blown fire erupted. I combusted into a blazing camp fire, flames infused with uncontainable love and explosive supernatural power from on high.

In an instant, Jesus took me into Himself and I was one with Him. We swiftly ascended to a high place. My arms and legs were fully extended, outstretched as if logs blazing with fire. I was the campfire burning in Jesus. We went high and I didn't feel afraid of the heights, I felt completely secure in Jesus.

From a secure place in Jesus, looking down I saw Australia covered in the same multi-coloured, multi-cultural feathers belonging to the angel. Only now these colours were embedded in the land. They were the colours and reflection of the ochre colours that lay within the lands. I could see all the colours and shades of white, cream, yellow, orange, brown, red dust and black. The colours represented the diverse skin colours of the diverse people groups in Australia.

A glory light moved across our nation, supernaturally calling out and drawing out the purity, maturity, humility and diversity of his Bride. I realised it was the breath of God blowing across the landscape. It highlighted each skin colour one at a time. It highlighted and ignited the diverse Australian bride, like no other. From the brightness of the light resounded this message: 'come alive, come alive!'

I could hear and feel the warmth of His words 'love like no other'. There is none as fair as you. He was speaking life and love over His beloved Bride.

Just as He did with me, Jesus leaned down, close over the continent of Australia and began to breathe on this land mass. As He began to blow, the landscape became kindling surrendered under the breath of God. As Jesus blew, sparks ignited and the land combusted into a striking campfire. In a split second the land mass of Australia erupted into a blazing camp fire.

Jesus looked at me, His eyes were flames of fire and in that moment, it was like eternal fire washed through me and consumed my all.

The blue flames, and the white flames burned with piercing fire of the one who is the all-consuming fire (see Hebrews 12:29).

In the flickering flames of Jesus eyes, I could clearly see the reflection of the many ochre colours of the people groups' skin. Jesus eyes were on His multi-coloured Australian Bride. Burning within me was the love of Father God for His diverse Australian Bride. I am forever changed. His flaming eyes were a reflection of the many nations and skin tones in the land of Australia.

Australia, you carry my imprint, my footprint, the blueprint of my love. Australia you carry the diverse imprint of my beloved bride. Arise my radiant Bride, AS ONE!

I believe The Lord is establishing us in new dimensions of Ephesians 3:18 the depth, height, width and breadth of His love that draws us to Himself and into greater dimensions of unity.

> [14] For this reason I kneel before the Father, [15] from whom every family in heaven and on earth derives its name. [16] I pray that out of his glorious riches he may strengthen you with power through his Spirit in your inner being, [17] so that Christ may dwell in your hearts through faith. And I pray that you, being rooted and established in love, [18] may have power, together with all the Lord's holy people, to grasp how **wide** and **long** and **high** and **deep** is the love of Christ, [19] and to know this love that surpasses knowledge—that you may be filled to the measure of all the fullness of God (Ephesians 3:14-19 NIV).

I believe in Australia, we will see gatherings, small and large in 'camp- fire' like settings, in families, communities, outdoors and indoor 'fire houses.'

These campfire gatherings will be marked with fiery Jesus encounters and manifestations of miracles. They will come through the lightning bolt power charged with Father's love. They will come as the flaming word of God is sent forth from the mouths of living sacrifices, like swords of the Lord.

God took me to 1 Kings 18, the account of Elijah on Mt Carmel when Elijah assembled twelve stones, which represented the twelve tribes of Israel.   These twelve stones while representing the twelve tribes of Israel spoke to me of Australia and its diverse people groups. He then called on God who sent supernatural fire from heaven that consumed the water, stones, sacrifice and the soil (see verse 38).

As the cultures and skin colours converge, and come together as one living sacrifice, the supernatural fire of God will fall.

We recognise that in this account many still chose to worship their idols, but I believe in this era, the supernatural fire of God will blaze its trail upon us and the people will unequivocally turn to God and be set ablaze as His burning ones.

In the encounter, as the fire over Australia grew hotter and the flames rose higher, the sparks bounced and danced, jumping high up in the sky. In the Spirit, I saw red hot embers sent out like flaming arrows from the land of Australia. The messengers of fire, the angels of the Lord gravitated to the embers. Angels caught and transported them into the nations of the Great Southland of the Holy Spirit and back to Israel. As the breath of God blew, it was the wind of His Spirit that supernaturally carried the embers alive, out into the airways where they were sent. The live sparks travelled across the airways and into the airspace of the Islands of the South Pacific, part of The Great South Lands of the Holy Spirit.

In the Spirit realm I heard the shofar, then I heard the shofar with the didgeridoo, the clapsticks, the conch-shell and the drums all together. It was a glorious sound.

I strongly sensed He was looking for somewhere to land the live sparks sent out from Australia. As the sparks landed, an instant campfire blazed a trail across these nations.

The breath of God is blowing over this nation to set it ablaze causing it to fix its gaze upon the one who breathes life into the land, and into the people. He is preparing to launch Australia into the nations like a fiery arrow from His quiver sent to accomplish His will.

During 2020 and 2021 the Lord has been fashioning His Australian Bride to unite colour and creed, tongue and tribe, denominations and generations as ONE in the nations. In the midst of the turmoil, we have seen a strong *coming together* of these streams, particularly in prayer across the world. There has been such a strong sense of coming together, into the One Diverse Bride in purity and humility of heart.
Many facets of Father reflected through many people groups, a reflection of the *many as one*. There has been a convergence of streams into one.

We have already seen the beginnings of this in the National Solemn Assembly led by Indigenous Fathers and Mothers, partnering with Non-Indigenous national leaders from many streams. We came together, converging for one purpose to humble ourselves, pray and seek His face and turn from our wicked ways so that God will forgive us and heal our land (see 2 Chronicles 7:14).

In the midst of unrest and racial upheaval, this demonstration of Kingdom power and love and focussed faith will unleash the power of heaven to overthrow the kingdoms of this world.

I encourage Intercessors and watchman warriors, along with all of us to fast, pray, and travail to birth us into this new and powerful dimension of oneness.

I believe out of Australia will rise A *'Remnant Army of Reformers'* to lead the charge of the 'one new man' marked as one with God and one with another!

As the remnant army of reformers lead the *'new breed of burning ones'* and as God's power and authority thunders through the land and its *'united and ignited'* diverse people groups, I believe:

➢ That a *'greater works power surge'* of purity and authority is being released into the sold out; set apart; living sacrifice remnant. Those that have fortified conviction and character, who are seasoned-in-combat, will be sent to confront and conquer the kingdoms of this world.

➢ We will see a strong convergence of diverse streams into unity and oneness like we haven't seen. This will include watchman, gatekeepers, intercessors, five-fold, and seven mountain warriors. The ecclesia will emerge as one combat unit.

➢ We will begin to see the rise of the First Nations five-fold like never before. Black and white running together in humility and maturity to advance the Kingdom of God as one united force to be reckoned with.

➢ These five-fold combinations will function in the community campfire, *'fire-house'* settings, creating *'hot-houses-of-heaven';* environments where people will encounter Jesus. *'Hot-houses'* where people will feed on the word of God, combust and ignite others to gather around their own campfire. The fiery word of God will spread like wild-fire.

> ➢ The Lord is fashioning His diverse Australian Bride to *'unite and ignite'* with ancient flame to reign in this new era.

I believe God's destiny for Australia, South Pacific Islands and New Zealand is to be unified fire sticks set ablaze with revival fires, bringing transformation and reformation to the nations. I hear the Lord say *'Australia you are my burning one, it has now begun!'*

Decree with me:

Your Holy Fire has come upon me Lord, I decree it has burned up the old mindsets, old wineskin, and old ways of thinking, leading, governing and trading. I decree it is replaced with new mindsets, new *'mind-skins,'* new wine and new strategies.

I decree, the holy fire of God has back-burned, right through my historical generational bloodline, cleansing me of all cursing.

I decree I am now free of age old cursing. I decree it has been burned away. I am cleansed by the blood of the lamb, I am a new creation.
I decree that God is now bringing me forth into generational blessing. I decree I am being filled afresh with new wine and new strategies.

I decree that I have been set ablaze with an eternal flame. Your breath has ignited a flame in me for eternal reign. I am your eternal torch.

Lord Jesus, I decree I am your burning one!

Decrees over You from Isaiah 61:1-7

I decree that The Spirit of the Sovereign LORD is upon you,
I decree you are anointed by The Lord
I decree that you boldly proclaim good news to the poor.
I decree that you are empowered to bind up and heal the brokenhearted
I decree freedom for the captives
I decree release from darkness for the prisoners

I decree that this is the year of the LORD's favor. I decree favor over your life right now, In Jesus name!
I decree the day of vengeance of our God
I decree comfort for all who mourn
I decree the release of the Lord's provision to all those who grieve in Zion—
I decree a crown of beauty is bestowed upon you, instead of ashes; I decree the oil of joy is all over you, instead of mourning
I decree a garment of praise is upon you, the spirit of despair has disappeared and gone.
I decree you are called oaks of righteousness, a planting of the LORD; I decree that you display His splendor.

I decree that ancient ruins are rebuilt, and the places long devastated are now restored.

I decree that the ruined cities that have been devastated for generations are renewed.

I decree they are no longer in ruins, no longer in devastation. Generations restored, rebuilt and renewed, in Jesus name.
I decree strangers will shepherd your flocks, foreigners will work your fields and vineyards.

I decree you are called priests of the LORD, you are named ministers of our God.
I decree you feed on the wealth of nations, and in their riches you now boast.

I decree no more shame, receive your double portion,
I decree no more disgrace, rejoice now in your inheritance.
I decree that the double portion be released into your life. It is your inheritance in your land.

I decree everlasting joy is now yours.

I Decree that you have stepped into a John 14:12 greater works and you will see a manifestation of the miraculous not seen before.

I Decree that you are empowered with a **Matthew 10:8 anointing to** heal the sick, raise the dead, cleanse the lepers, cast out demons with supernatural power and authority.

Decree over Australia:

Australia, you are birthing Kingdom blueprints, plans and purposes. There will be multiple birthings into the land for such a time as this.

Australia, you are set ablaze in new ways, you are entering new dimensions of the Kingdom of heaven.

The fire of God is bringing forth the gold and an end time harvest in this nation Australia.

Australia, you have been set ablaze with an eternal flame that will not be snuffed out. Australia, you are set ablaze with the eternal fire of God.

Lord release the *'greater works power surge'* of purity and authority through your remnant in this land.

Streams converge into unity and oneness like never before.

Ecclesia arise as one combat unit in this nation! First Nations five-fold rise up empowered to function in your mantle.

Campfire gatherings ignite; Fire-Houses erupt; and Hot Houses of Heaven be established across the nation. The Lord is raising up a new breed of burning ones for Jesus.

Diverse Australian Bride, *'unite and ignite'* with the ancient flame of everlasting love and reign.

Australia, you are His burning one!

Chapter 9

Refined and Reformed

"But who will be able to stand up to that coming? Who can survive his appearance? He'll be like white-hot fire from the smelter's furnace. He'll be like the strongest lye soap at the laundry. He'll take his place as a refiner of silver, as a cleanser of dirty clothes. He'll scrub the Levite priests clean, refine them like gold and silver, until they're fit for GOD, fit to present offerings of righteousness. Then, and only then, will Judah and Jerusalem be fit and pleasing to GOD, as they used to be in the years long ago". (Malachi 3:3 MSG)

"Since we have received such great promises "let us cleanse ourselves from everything that contaminates and defiles body and spirit, and bring [our] consecration to completeness in the [reverential] fear of God". (2 Corinthians 7:1 AMPC)

" Now in a large house there are not only vessels and objects of gold and silver, but also vessels and objects of wood and of earthenware, and some are for honourable (noble, good) use and some for dishonourable (ignoble, common. Therefore, if anyone cleanses himself from these things [which are dishonourable—disobedient, sinful], he will be a vessel for honour, sanctified [set apart for a special purpose and], useful to the Master, prepared for every good work". (2 Tim 2: 20, 21 AMP)

I heard the Lord say these two words to me:

Refined and Reformed!

As I sought the Lord on this, suddenly it made perfect sense! He is coming back for a bride without spot, wrinkle or blemish. I believe we are in a season of being refined within and reformed for what is to come. We have to be refined and reformed on the inside before we become empowered and equipped to transform and reform the outside world around us.

So I looked up the meaning of these two words and this is what was revealed:

Definition of Refined:

With impurities or unwanted elements having been removed by processing

Synonyms of Refined:

purified · pure · clarified · clear · sifted · polished

Definition of Reformed:

Having been changed in such a way as to be improved.

Having relinquished, or to give up an immoral way of life, or a self-destructive lifestyle.

I believe this is a timely word from the Lord. God is wanting to remove impurities from us, even the impurities that we don't know we have. He is doing a deep purification in this new era. He is using this time to purify His people, the hungry ones, and the ones who are awake.

It's an opportunity to invite Him into our secret struggles, to cleanse, deliver and to heal us, to restore us from destructive behaviour and a destructive way of life. God is not wanting to reprimand us, no. He lovingly desires to deliver, cleanse and heal us.

I'm going to make a decree right from the outset of this chapter. I invite you to agree with it and receive it too

Decree:

I declare and decree that in these times, I am being refined and reformed to come out purified to walk in greater measure of Holy Spirit's power and authority, for your Glory Lord. Amen!

The Lord spoke some words to me that I have heard Him say before in different encounters. I believe I was hearing these words again, in the context of being refined and reformed, because they are important words to hear in these times.

Fire to Burn-Up and Fire to Bring-Forth

Where there is refining there is fire

I heard the Lord say this about the fire of God:

'It is fire to burn up and fire to bring forth!'

'There are areas of your life that have been ruled by the enemy up to now, and the Lord would say 'No more, I AM blazing a trail through the chambers of your heart, through the fibres of your being, setting a fire in your bones, for I am a consuming fire'

For our "God is a consuming fire." (Hebrews 12:29 NIV)

His refining fire is a consuming fire 🔥 . This fire is not like any fire we know on planet earth. This fire is fire that consumes every single thing that does not totally align with the holiness and purity of heaven.

He again reminded me of these words spoken in another encounter I had, only this time it yielded a different revelation:

I am burning away the old – the old mindsets, old wine skin, old ways of leading, governing, trading and aligning. I am burning up the old to birth my original plan and purpose for your life, in more of its fullness. Fire to burn up and fire to bring forth. I am back-burning to the time of your birth, to bring you forth in my glory.

I am back-burning through the historic generational line, to rid you of age old cursing, to then bring you forth in generational blessing and to fill you with new era wine.

I am back-burning to birth a fresh new move of My Spirit across this land through my refined and reformed burning ones.

Fire to burn up

2 Timothy, 2 Corinthians and Malachi highlight at least 3 compelling reasons to submit to the refining fire of God to be refined and reformed:

1) So we are vessels of honour fit for the Master's use

2) Out of a place of gratitude for being beneficiaries of such extraordinary promises

3) So we can be fit and pleasing to Him

Vessels of Honour:

The Lord wants to cleanse and purify us, to refine us, so we can be noble vessels of honour fit for the Master's use.

> "Now in a large house there are not only vessels *and* objects of gold and silver, but also vessels *and* objects of wood and of earthenware, and some are for honourable (noble, good) use and some for dishonourable (ignoble, common. Therefore, if anyone cleanses himself from these *things* [which are dishonourable—disobedient, sinful], he will be a **vessel for honour**, sanctified [set apart for a special purpose and], useful to the Master, prepared for every good work". (2 Tim 2: 20, 21 AMP)

We get to choose whether we are a vessel of honour, fit for the Master's use, by whether or not we cleanse ourselves and are willing to let the Lord's refining fire purify us.

The beneficiaries of extraordinary promises:

Paul in 2 Corinthians masterly details, "the surpassing glory of the new covenant" (3:16,17) "the eternal glory awaiting us" (4:17), "our eternal house in heaven not made with human hands that we will be clothed in" (5:1) and our "new creation nature" (5:17).

In the light of these extraordinary promises Paul writes,

"Since we have received such great promises "let us cleanse ourselves from everything that contaminates *and* defiles body and spirit, and bring [our] consecration to completeness in the [reverential] fear of God". (2 Corinthians 7:1 AMPC)

In the NASB version Paul speaks of "perfecting holiness in the fear of God". (2 Corinthians 7:1 NASB).

Paul saw the "perfecting of holiness' and "fear of God" as inseparable. The fear and reverent awe of God were the motivation for perfecting holiness.

Fit and pleasing to the Lord:

The Prophet Malachi asks the question, who will survive His coming? Who will survive His appearing? Because when He comes he will be like a white-hot fire from the smelter's furnace. Those He refines and purifies will then, and only then, be fit and pleasing to Him.

"But who will be able to stand up to that coming? Who can survive his appearance? He'll be like white-hot fire from the smelter's furnace. He'll be like the strongest lye soap at the laundry. He'll take his place as a refiner of silver, as a cleanser of dirty clothes. He'll scrub the Levite priests clean, refine them like gold and silver, until they're fit for GOD, fit to present offerings of righteousness. Then, and only then, will Judah and Jerusalem be fit and pleasing to GOD, as they used to be in the years long ago". (See Malachi 3:3)

The writer to the Hebrews also highlights the explosive fact that "The Lord is a consuming fire" (see Hebrews 12:29 NIV)

I want to encourage you to get ready to enter new dimensions, to be set ablaze in new ways, for the Kingdom of God to bring in the end time harvest. Get ready to be refined by fire and reformed to bring transformation. That looks like something.

For you, that might look like going out into your family, into your neighbourhood, into your community. For some it will be to go out into Australia, for others it will be go out into the nations that the Lord tells you to, whether it is physically travelling to those nations or ministering powerfully through the airwaves of technology and on zoom.

We are called to release whatever it is that you carry of the Lord and His Kingdom. It could be God's nature, His kindness, gentleness, or his compassion for the lost, for women, or men, or widows, or the poor, the less fortunate, or for the children. It could be that he wants you to be a voice for the voiceless, those suffering abuse, or those being sex trafficked.

These are some causes that are marked with the fingerprint of Father God that you carry, and that's part of the Kingdom within you. He has placed that inside of you and He wants you to give it out, to show the people around you that part of Father God that He has given you to share.

It could be His gifts of intercession, He calls for the watchman warriors to come up higher by going deeper into intimacy with Him.

The blueprints and plans could be the dreams you hold in your heart, or the visions the Lord has given to you in the secret place. The things revealed to you when you are alone with Him; spending time with Him in prayer; or communion with the Lord. It could be through encounters with God; or prophetic words you've had. These are the things the Lord wants you to birth and bring forth, in your life and to your sphere of influence in the world around you.

Let me encourage you to pull out any prophetic words you've had spoken over your life. If it resonates with you, contend for it, believe for it, see it and decree it over your life. Let the Lord do his refining work in you to burn up the stuff that hinders you, and burn up the stuff that stops you from stepping into your destiny, that stops you having the courage or the confidence to be bold, share the gospel and be all that you are called to be.

The Lord reminded me of these words he recently spoke concerning another prophetic word that He gave me:

'I am setting ablaze within you an eternal flame. You will become my eternal torch. My breath will ignite a flame in you for eternal reign.'

His breath sets coals aglow, and a flame goes forth from his mouth (Job 41:12 NASB)

In Job 41 we read that the breath of God sets coals on fire and flames come forth from his mouth. This flame, this fire, is the breath of the Almighty. It is no ordinary fire. It has the potential to both purify, and ignite great passion and zeal in the heart of believers so they can become 'burning ones' who ignite those they come in contact with.

Bride – He is purifying you to display His splendour through you (see Isaiah 61:3)!! He is preparing us to take our seat at the right hand of the Father (see Ephesians 2:6), in power that we haven't tapped into yet for us to co-rule and reign with Christ in a greater way. To govern in our world, like we haven't done before, in greater authority, with greater power!

He said to me something similar to what He said in a recent word:

I am preparing you my bride. Cleansing, purifying, removing and re-constructing - Why? To re-create and impregnate his ready ones; His burning ones with Kingdom blueprints, plans and purposes to be birthed into this land, in these times.

I believe this is all part of the refining and reforming that he is highlighting today.

In the refining, we are to surrender the bits in us that were never meant to be there. Surrender our stinky heart attitudes, our sin, the things we struggle with, the bits that don't line up with the word of God, and God's truth of who He says we are.

Hebrews 12:1 tells us:

> "*Therefore, since we are surrounded by such a great cloud of witnesses, let us throw off everything that hinders, and the sin that so easily entangles. And let us run with perseverance the race marked out for us*" (Hebrews 12:1 NIV).

I believe that amongst the great cloud of witnesses – are our saved loved ones that have gone before us. These Include our First Nations family, pastors and leaders watching over us, cheering us on as we run the race, barracking for us as we fight the good fight of faith.

> Fight the good fight of faith, lay hold on eternal life, to which you were also called and have confessed the good confession in the presence of many witnesses. (1 Timothy 6:12 NKJV)

Until we can confidently proclaim 2 Timothy 4:7

> I have fought the good (worthy, honourable, and noble) fight, I have finished the race, I have kept (firmly held) the faith (AMPC)

Sometimes we aren't aware of what entangles us.

Activation:

I want to encourage you to ask Holy Spirit to show you the things that are holding you back. Take a moment now and ask:

- 'Holy Spirit show me what is entangling me?
- What is hindering my intimacy with you Lord?
- Lord what do I need to throw off today? What do you want to burn up in me, to refine me to be a light for you Lord Jesus?

Now listen and wait to hear, feel or sense what Holy Spirit is saying to you. He might show you in a picture, a vision or through an impression, or scripture.

Let me encourage you to throw off bitterness that you may have deep in your heart towards another person self-bitterness towards yourself, temptation, gossip, slander, shame, and torment. Throw off condemnation, comparison and competition.

Once the Holy Spirit has revealed to you what you need to throw off. Give it to Him in an act of faith, or a prophetic act and ask: Lord what will you give me in return?

Now listen and wait to hear, feel or sense what Holy Spirit is saying to you. He might show you in a picture, a vision or through an impression, or scripture.

He is a good, good Father and He will surely give you something good.

- When He does, make note of it. Write down what the Lord said He will give you in return.

It is a promise that He is revealing to you personally for you to take hold of. I encourage you to look up what the word of God says about the message the Lord gave you in exchange for your shame, anger, frustration, disappointment, guilt, fear, or whatever it is you are giving to Him today.

It's time to declare *truth and truce*. Determine to *run together* in covenant relationship with one another in oneness, championing one another. What a wonderful thing it is to champion someone! Friends, this is a call to *new dimensions of purity and unity* as we go low surrendering to our Lord in humility!

God is calling us to an internal cleansing, to refine and purify us, and establish us in the fear of the Lord. He is refining us to be reformed to then release reformation through us into our families, our communities, our town, and our region. If we *'all'* do this – it will transform your town, community or city. It will transform your region and it will transform our nation! Amen!

You are vital to God's plan in the nation. It starts with you, it starts with me. Let's take responsibility to position ourselves before the Lord and allow Him to purify us.

As you are *refined and reformed* in the '*Going Low*' and '*Going Deep*;' as you receive divine *revelation*; as you are *empowered* by the Spirit of the Lord; you are *equipped* to '*rise*' with High Ranking authority – because you've gone through the refining fire, and rid yourself of the hindering things. As you have allowed Holy Spirit to transform and reform you on the inside, you will be in a position to war and annihilate the enemy with your prayer and intercession. You will be positioned to sustain the anointing, to carry and release His Glory where-ever you go, and then '*release*' to others the gifts, graces, and revelations God has given to you.

As we do this, we will see His Glory increased throughout the land in this new era. Glory will saturate His people with awe-striking miracles as the power of His hand is released upon the earth, and we begin to see Habakkuk 2:14 the knowledge of His Glory cover the earth as the waters cover the sea.

The Lord reminded me of this phrase He said to me much earlier:

Large land masses will be struck with My goodness, my fast flowing love will be like a flood. No longer will I be denied, souls will come flooding in.

I believe these are the times we are coming into, a time of great harvest and miracles. This is what we are being '*refined and reformed*' for. To be equipped and empowered – *ready* for the move of God that is coming. To be ready for the magnitude of the harvest that is upon us, *ready* to go out in power, and to bring light to the darkness. Be ready to see God move *miraculously* through you, for His glory.

Could I encourage you to let Him *refine* and *reform* you! To *go low,* in greater humility before the throne of grace. *Go deep* into the secret place in intimacy with Jesus and Father God. Seek Him and ask Him to take you into the realm of *covenant oneness with him,* preparing your hands for battle, preparing you for war. Let nothing distract you from Him. Let Him equip you and empower you, by His Spirit, to *rise up* in your God ordained high ranking authority to rule and reign in power with Christ, from your seat in the heavenly realms. To govern from victory, and smite the enemies plans.

Could I encourage you to *release* and share all that God imparts and downloads to you! All the Kingdom blueprints He gives you for the times ahead, at the right time, in His timing. Be bold and courageous, and *expect* the miraculous in quantities, in magnitude, and in dimensions and ways that will shock the world. *Expect* this move of God to cause a flood of souls. Partner with Holy Spirit, partner with this word to see God miraculously transform our nation to see reformation begin in our nation, let us pray this in. Declare the word of God, decree it. Proclaim the gospel every chance you get. *Expect* people to respond to it, *expect* them to be saved, healed and delivered. Get ready for the harvest that's coming.

I feel the Lord saying release My *glory* as you *rise* and *take dominion* and *govern the earth.*

> Proverbs 8:16 TPT says:
> *I empower princes to rise and take dominion and generous ones to govern the earth. ... Amen!*

Prayer

Lord Release the fire of God in this place, release your refining fire, the *fire to burn* up and the *fire to bring forth.*

For God is a consuming fire! We surrender in the reverential fear of the Lord and say, Lord take us deep, take us deep into you, into your presence, and consume us Holy Spirit.

Lord we release the consuming fire of God and the wind of the Spirit - to catch and spread the flames. *Refine and reform us.* Let the wind of your Spirit blow through us blazing a trail through the chambers of our heart, cleansing, refining us from the inside out. Lord as we surrender more of ourselves to you right now, help us to bow low before you in greater humility Abba Father. Release us into the deeper realms of intimacy with you, take us with you now, into the place of covenant oneness in the Spirit realm with you.

Show us what that looks like Lord. To know you more, your heart, your mind, your blueprints and plan, in a greater way. To commune with you on a deeper level, take us there now Lord. Let us encounter you in new ways, new dimension of encounter, open our eyes to the angelic realm. Take us so deep that we cross-over from one place in the natural realm, to a new place in the Spirit realm. Let us cross over into a new depth with you, to hear your heartbeat.

Give us ears to hear what the Spirit is saying in this place, let ears pop open now, in Jesus mighty name. Ears, be unblocked to hear Father God speak. Let eyes be opened to see what you see Father.

Transfer your plans and purposes to us, impart to us your wisdom, your ways, as we declare our unwavering love for you, Abba Father. Oh Jesus, we respond to your call to come away with you, again and again in Jesus wonderful name.

My Prayer for You:

I ask Lord, that you release this son/daughter into *deeper* and *greater encounters* with you. Release them into the new level. I call you forth into the new level. I call them into their destiny. I ask for clarity for those who are not clear on their destiny. Release clarity now.

Father I thank you for allowing us to commune on a deeper level with you. You are ever faithful, you are moving through the chambers of hearts refining us, reforming us, and you are speaking to your people.

Lord I ask you to impart the *faith of* God, not just faith in God but an impartation of the supernatural Faith of God right now, to see your dreams, the prophetic words spoken over you be fulfilled. May Father God impart to you right now. Lord, supernaturally ignite in you, the dreams, the vision, the blueprints on His heart and mind.

I pray every dream is ignited. I pray the Lord grant you courage to take up the baton to run your race, to say this is mine, to claim it, embrace it, and rise in the authority of it.

May the Lord help you to determine in your heart and Spirit that nothing is going to entangle you, hinder you, or stop you, in Jesus name. Nothing will cause you to back down from what He has for you. Decree: Lord you have my 'yes'.

Lord I pray that you release that impartation of faith and courage right now that can only come by your Holy Spirit.
Holy Spirit release the *ruach* breath of God on each one engaged in this prayer now. Some of you will actually feel the breath of God, some may not really feel anything but I encourage you to take hold of this right now by faith.

Holy Spirit touch you right now, right where you are. Awaken that destiny inside of you. Where dreams have been asleep, dormant or stuck or in-waiting, I speak to the seed of that dream and say awaken, awake!

I ask that you Holy Spirit would wake each one up. Dreams wake up, destiny unlock, destiny awake. I call you forth in the name of Jesus.

Lord I thank you that you are faithful to complete the good work you have started (see Philippians 1:6), faithful to watch over your word to perform your word over their lives (see Jeremiah 1:12). What you have started you will finish. Lord I thank you right now, we celebrate your goodness, your faithfulness, your unending love, we celebrate who you are and we celebrate each other and who we are in you.

Blessing:

Lord I speak a blessing over each person right now. Lord bless them with favour. Just as Jesus grew in stature and had favour with God and favour with man (see Luke 2:52). Lord bless them with this same favour with God and favour with man. As in Deuteronomy 28:6 I declare you will be blessed when you go in and blessed when you go out. You will be blessed in the city, you will be blessed in the country. Lord bless them as they move in and out of the city and in and out of the country. Bless them with heavenly wisdom. Beloved friend, I pray that you are prospering in every way and that
you continually enjoy good health, just as your soul is prospering (3 John 1:2). Lord bless them with prosperity and divine health, bless them with healing and restoration, bless their relationships with family, restore family relationships, bless them to encounter you in mighty ways, bless them with angelic encounters.

Whatever has held them back be *broken* off their life, that whatever work of the enemy, any sickness that has hindered them or stopped them. We speak to sickness and say 'shift and lift' in Jesus name. Lord break the power of every evil work in the name of Jesus. Lord I thank you that you are lifting them up, that they are rising with you, rising on wings like eagles. Lord release healing power to surge through your body like fire, burning up sickness, burn up disease, burn up abnormalities, burn up foreign cells, burn up cysts, burn up abnormal lumps, burn up malfunction in organs, burn like fire through your veins, your arteries, your organs, your bones, right now in Jesus mighty name. I speak to a spirit of infirmity and command you to leave, go now. Go back to the pit of hell in Jesus name. Release healing power in Jesus name. I command your body's insides to line up with the eternal truth of God that by His stripes you are healed (see Isaiah 53:5).

I bless you to come in and join with the army arising. You are now part of this wave, this birthing, this miraculous move of God and you are going to make an impact in your town, your region, your nation. Father I thank you for that, I bless each one right now, in the mighty name of Yeshua Hamashiach, Jesus Christ. Amen and amen.

To transform a life of fear, shame, and guilt TO freedom, healing and wholeness

Email: Peter or Katie Dunstan @
breakfreeaust@gmail.com

Visit amazon.com.au (Australia) or
amazon.com (Other Countries)

To access:

'Healing Wounded Hearts: Holy Spirit Directed Inner Healing' by Peter and Katherine Dunstan.

Chapter 10

Remnant Army of Reformers Arise!

"Then Zerubbabel the son of Shealtiel, and Joshua the son of Jehozadak, the high priest, with all the remnant of the people, obeyed the voice of the LORD their God and the words of Haggai the prophet, just as the LORD their God had sent him. And the people showed reverence for the LORD". (Haggai 1:12 NASB)

So the LORD stirred up the spirit of Zerubbabel the son of Shealtiel, governor of Judah, and the spirit of Joshua the son of Jehozadak, the high priest, and the spirit of all the remnant of the people; and they came and worked on the house of the LORD of armies, their God, (Haggai 1:14 NASB)

I will once more shake the heavens (demonic realms) and earth (the realm of men), the sea and the dry land … and I will fill this house with Glory. (Haggai 2:6-7 NASB)
I will overturn royal thrones and shatter the power of the foreign kingdoms … (Haggai 2:22 NIV)

(Haggai 1:12; Haggai 1:14; Haggai 2:6-7; Haggai 2:22)

$\mathcal{A}$ "Remnant Army of Reformers' is rising to reclaim the land, their mission is transformation and reformation. They will restore, rebuild, and reform the church, as it is known today, as a prelude to ushering in the Kingdom of God. A special unit SWAT team is about to storm heaven and go out to reclaim the land of this nation, Australia, and the nations.

In the coming revival that will sweep the nations, I believe God has been training, equipping and preparing a remnant army to rise and be instrumental in revival, reformation and transformation. These are three ancient keys to the move of God.

Revival:

The first of these three is an awakening of the church. This involves the church returning to its first love, and Holy Spirit being poured out in power. This will result in a mighty harvest of souls and supernatural signs and wonders on a scale never seen before.

Reformation:

In the 1500s we had the Protestant Reformation that swept through Europe. It changed the face and structure of the church forever. I believe a reformation is coming that will eclipse the Protestant Reformation in scale and impact.
This reformation will restore, rebuild and reshape the church. It will involve a shift from what we know as the Pastor based leadership models to Apostolic leadership teams including prophets, evangelists, teachers and pastors.

These Apostolic leadership teams will unite and align to bring unity to the Body of Christ and equip the saints for the work of ministry. The authority of the Apostle will be restored and the "ecclesia" will arise with great authority to shift spiritual atmospheres, and pull down demonic strongholds over regions and nations.

Transformation:

The present local church focus will shift to a focus on the Kingdom of God, and the will of God being done on earth as it is in heaven in a much greater way. This focus will involve discipling nations and the institutions in the nations. The Kingdom of God does not simply involve the local church. The Kingdom of God is an all-encompassing Kingdom that involves the political systems, the education systems, media etc. With revival sweeping the nations and signs and wonders filling social media, the institutions of society will be transformed by empowered Christians moving into the institutions in society as leaven and aligning them with the Kingdom of God.

> "Nations will come to your light and Kings to the brightness of your rising" (Isaiah 60:3 NASB)

> "And in the days of those kings the God of heaven will set up a kingdom which will never be destroyed, and *that* kingdom will not be left for another people; it will crush and put an end to all these kingdoms, but it will itself endure forever". (Daniel 2:44 NIV)

Vision:

In a vision I saw people in a navy coloured uniform. Written on the uniform in white letters was the word 'Reform'. It had a 'military' sense about it. A specialised taskforce unit, like a 'S.W.A.T Team.' The sense I had was that this 'S.W.A.T Team' would be made up of Intercessor, Gate Keepers, Watchman Warriors, Apostles, Prophets, Evangelists, Pastors and Teachers and their teams, all working together as one unit. They were running in a single file, one behind the other, all in sync, all in unison. Armed and running up, out of a rough land gully. SWAT stands for Special Weapons and Tactics. A SWAT team is an elite unit and force to be reckoned with, used for exceptional situations that require increased firepower or specialized tactics. Each one in a SWAT unit have undergone special training and have access to an arsenal of weaponry, armour and surveillance devices beyond standard-issued armed force gear. Much of this gear comes in the form of military surplus.

While all SWAT officers are expert marksmen with in-depth training in close combat, most play a specialized role within the team. SWAT officers act as paramilitary units that tackle situations beyond the capability of conventional armed forces. SWAT officers are armed with weapons of higher calibre than most officers, such as machine guns, shotguns and sniper rifles.

I believe God is raising up a 'Remnant Army of Reformers' with specialised roles, who are single-minded, focussed on Christ, and the Kingdom of God. I believe He is releasing a Spirit of Reformation into this nation! He is equipping the troops, getting them ready to be deployed into the nation, and the nations. 'Transform' and 'Reform' is their mission.

This was surrounded with a sense that, one assignment for the Reformers is to drive a stake into this land, Australia.
I heard the Lord say:

'I am reclaiming the land'. 'As I stake the land I am declaring *reformation in this nation.*'

I believe the book of Haggai is a prophetic picture of what God is doing in terms of reforming the church and transforming the nations.

In the Book of Haggai, the prophet was turning the attention of the people from building their own house, to building the temple of the Lord.

> *"This is what the* LORD *of armies says: 'This people says, "The time has not come, the time for the house of the* LORD *to be rebuilt." Then the word of the* LORD *came by Haggai the prophet, saying, "Is it time for you yourselves to live in your panelled houses while this house remains desolate?"* (Haggai 1:2-4 NASB)

Today the Lord is overturning and removing personal agendas to build your own temple, name or ministry. He is calling His troops into alignment with the Kingdom blueprint of heaven, to rebuild the temple (the church) and bring reformation to the nations. Self-glorifying kingdoms will be overturned in these times.

In Haggai the reformers and temple builders are described as a "remnant."

"Then Zerubbabel the son of Shealtiel, and Joshua the son of Jehozadak, the high priest, with all the remnant of the people, obeyed the voice of the LORD their God and the words of Haggai the prophet, just as the LORD their God had sent him. And the people showed reverence for the LORD". (Haggai 1:12 NASB)

Today God is raising up a remnant to bring forth this rebuilding of the temple. I believe He is raising up a remnant to bring forth this reformation to the nation. I see this as a prototype of reformation coming to us in these times.

So the LORD stirred up the spirit of Zerubbabel the son of Shealtiel, governor of Judah, and the spirit of Joshua the son of Jehozadak, the high priest, and the spirit of all the remnant of the people; and they came and worked on the house of the LORD of armies, their God, (Haggai 1:14 NASB)

The temple God is building in these days is not a physical temple in Jerusalem , but a spiritual temple of living stones where God can dwell and manifest His glory in the earth. He is stirring us up to usher in revival, reformation and transformation to the nations.

"And coming to Him as to a living stone which has been rejected by people, but is choice and precious in the sight of God, you also, as living stones, are being built up as a spiritual house (temple) for a holy priesthood, to offer spiritual sacrifices that are acceptable to God through Jesus Christ." (1 Peter 2:4, 5 NASB)

Haggai tells us that the Lord will take this remnant and use them like a signet ring (Haggai 2:23 NASB).

> *On that day, declares the Lord I will take you, my servant ... and I will make you like my signet ring, for I have chosen you, declares the Lord Almighty.* (Haggai 2:23 NASB)

The signet ring represents authority. The remnant army rising will operate in Kingdom authority.

The glory of this restored, rebuilt and reformed temple (the church) will eclipse anything that has gone before it.

> *'Who is left among you who saw this temple in its former glory? And how do you see it now? Does it not seem to you like nothing in comparison?"* (Haggai 2:3 NASB)

It is this remnant, fortified with the authority and *faith of God*, sealed with the supernatural *love of the Father*, who others will look to in these times.

This is the remnant in uniform who *declare* and *release reformation in the nation*. This is the remnant to carry out the mission to

> *'Go up into the mountains (throne room) and bring down timber (heavenly revelation) and build the house (of God), so that I may take pleasure in it and be honoured, says the Lord.'* (Haggai 1:8 NIV). Additions in brackets are mine.

The Lord is highlighting to me, the mountain as a high place, an actual place in the spirit realm. It is the throne room, not a natural mountain top or natural building materials. This is a place of His glory where He is revered, honoured, and worshipped, in spirit and in truth. A place of purity, fear of the Lord, and holiness.

The building materials are supernatural tools, and Kingdom revelations, for you to access and impart into the nation.

I see fiery angels sent out into the nation, right alongside you as you are sent out. *In speaking of the angels, He says:*

'*He makes his angels spirits, and his servants, flames of fire.*' (Hebrews 1:7 NIV).

They are sent to join forces with you to ride the fiery wave of *reformation* that will sweep through this nation!! It will reproduce wave after wave, going out into the nation, and through ocean waters to crash onto the shores of other lands and nations.

> *… I will once more shake the heavens (demonic realms) and earth (the realm of men), the sea and the dry land … and I will fill this house with Glory...* (Haggai 2:6-7 NIV).

Australia, you are my remnant ones, set ablaze with the fire of my message of reformation. As the breath of God goes out into this nation, so goes the mighty wave of reformation!

Remnants in Scripture

God has never needed a majority to get his work done. Consider the thousands that followed Jesus throughout His ministry on earth. It was the 120 at the day of Pentecost to continue the work of Jesus on the earth. When the Holy Spirit fell in power, only a remnant remained to pick up the baton left behind by Jesus. This remnant changed the face of Christendom over centuries.

Genesis 18:26-33 CEV

The Genesis 18 remnant, where Abraham made a plea to save Sodom.

> [26] The Lord replied, "If I find fifty good people in Sodom, I will save the city to keep them from being killed." [27] Abraham answered, "I am nothing more than the dust of the earth. Please forgive me, Lord, for daring to speak to you like this. [28] But suppose there are only forty-five good people in Sodom. Would you still wipe out the whole city?" "If I find forty-five good people," the Lord replied, "I won't destroy the city." [29] "Suppose there are just forty good people?" Abraham asked. "Even for them," the Lord replied, "I won't destroy the city." [30] Abraham said, "Please don't be angry, Lord, if I ask you what you will do if there are only thirty good people in the city."
>
> "If I find thirty," the Lord replied, "I still won't destroy it." [31] Then Abraham said, "I don't have any right to ask you, Lord, but what would you do if you find only twenty?" "Because of them, I won't destroy the city," was the Lord's answer. [32] Finally, Abraham said, "Please don't get angry, Lord, if I speak just once more. Suppose you find only ten good people there."
>
> "For the sake of ten good people," the Lord told him, "I still won't destroy the city." [33] After speaking with Abraham, the Lord left, and Abraham went back home. (CEV)

The Genesis 18 remnant went from 50 to 45 to 40 to 30 to 20 and right down to 10. The Lord would spare a city if there was a remnant of righteous, upright and in right standing with God, innocent, good and true, Godly, decent men. God saved a city for the remnant. It doesn't take every person to draw down the fire and power of God. It only takes a remnant.

God is looking for the remnant. Are you a part of the remnant?

Consider Gideon, the Israelites had been oppressed by the Midianites for years. God raised up a young man who was fearful and suffered from an inferiority complex 'my clan is the weakest in Manasseh and I am the least in my family" (see Judges 6:15 NIV). He then told Gideon to strike down the Midianites. Gideon put a call out to four of the tribes of Israel to join him to destroy the oppressors. When they came armed ready to join him, God said, "You have too many men, I cannot deliver the Midianites into your hand or Israel will boast against me, "My own strength has saved me".

So Gideon said to the assembled army, "anyone who trembles with fear may turn back". 23,000 of the original 33,000 men went home and only 10,000 remained. The Lord said there are still too many (see Judges 7:4 NIV), Then God said, send home those who kneel down and lap like dogs when you go down to the water. All but 300 were sent home. From an army of 33,000 to a remnant army of 300. Why, so He would get the glory. God is looking for those spiritually aware.

This remnant army rising in these times will be fiery glory carriers. They will glorify the Lord. The glory will be all His.

God only needs a willing remnant, a remnant that is bold and courageous (see Joshua 1: 6, 7, 9 and 18 NIV) and does not tremble with fear. A remnant that is prepared and vigilant, who does not drop their armour weapons and lose focus, when they go down to the water to drink.

God is raising up such a bold, courageous, surrendered, and humble yet fierce, on fire for God remnant today, that He will use to bring revival, reformation and transformation to the nations.

Remnant Army of Reformers Arise! Intercessors, Gate Keepers, Watchman Warriors, Apostle, Prophets, Evangelists, Pastors and Teachers, put on your uniform. Ascend into the throne room to receive divine revelation. Release reformation to shatter the old foreign kingdoms that will be overthrown, and to see Jesus Kingdom enthroned in this nation, and the nations.

I will overturn royal thrones and shatter the power of the foreign kingdoms … (Haggai 2:22 NIV)

Kingdom Warriors Creed
By Peter Dunstan

In times of war or uncertainty there is a special breed of warrior (i) ready to answer Heaven's call. Common people with an uncommon desire to succeed. A remnant forged by adversity, we stand alongside mighty angel armies to serve our King and His Kingdom.

I am that warrior!

My inspiration is the legacy of those who have gone before me. Those who have conquered kingdoms, put foreign armies to flight, received back their dead by resurrection, were tortured, mocked, flogged, chained, imprisoned, stoned and sawn in two, and put to death in order that they might obtain a better resurrection (ii). They surround me in battle as a mighty cloud of witnesses (iii)

My loyalty to my King, my Country and my heavenly family is beyond reproach. I humbly serve as a guardian to my family, friends and nation, ready to defend those who are unable to defend themselves. I do not advertise the nature of my work, nor seek recognition for my actions, my crown (iv) and commendation (v) await me in heaven.

I voluntarily accept the inherent hazards of my calling, placing the welfare and security of others before my own.

I serve with honor on and off the battlefield. The ability to control my Spirit (vi) and my actions, regardless of circumstance, sets me apart from others. Uncompromising integrity is my standard. My character and honor are steadfast. My word is my bond. I do not allow myself to be entangled by sin (vii), nor do I engage in the affairs of civilian life (viii).

We expect to lead and be led. I take my orders from my Commander in Chief. His battle strategy comes to me through visions, dreams, prophecies and His Word. I will fight alongside my brothers and sisters to accomplish our mission. I lead by example in all situations.

I will never quit. I persevere (ix) and thrive on adversity. If knocked down, I will get back up, every time. I will draw on every remaining ounce of strength to protect my teammates and to accomplish our mission. I am never out of the fight.

I am clothed with unseen armour that never comes off (x). My weapons are not of human origin, but are divinely powerful to destroy defenses (xi). My mission is to destroy the works of my unseen enemy (xii), to bind him and plunder his goods (xiii) thus freeing those held captive and releasing those being held as prisoners(xiv).

We stay constantly alert and full of courage (xv). We demand discipline (xvi). The lives of my teammates and the success of our mission depend on me. My training is never complete.

We train for war and fight to win.

I stand ready to bring the full spectrum of divine weaponry to bear in order to achieve my mission and the goals established by my Commander in Chief, King Jesus. The execution of my duties will be swift and violent (xvii) when required. I have orders to heal the sick, raise the dead, caste out demons, cleanse lepers (xviii) and preach the all-conquering Kingdom of God (xix). We are required to disciple all the nations (xx).

Brave Kingdom Warriors have fought and died building the proud tradition and feared reputation that I am bound to uphold. In the worst of conditions, the legacy of my Commander in Chief and my teammates steadies my resolve and silently guides my every deed.

I WILL NOT FAIL, because my Commander in Chief has never failed.

(i)   2 Timothy 2:3, Philippians 2:25
(ii)   Hebrews 11:33-37
(iii)   Hebrews 12:1
(iv)   James 1:12, 2 Tim 4:8
(v)   Matthew 25:21
(vi)   Proverbs 16:32
(vii)   Hebrews 12:1
(viii)   2 Timothy 2:4 GNT
(ix)   James 1:3
(x)   Ephesians 6:13-17
(xi)   2 Corinthians 10:4
(xii)   1 John 3:8
(xiii)   Matthew 12:29
(xiv)   Isaiah 61:1
(xv)   Matthew 25:21
(xvi)   1 Corinthians 9:27
(xvii)   Proverbs 16:32
(xviii) Matthew 10:8

(xix)   Daniel 2:44

(xx)   Matthew 28:19

Adapted from the US Navy Seals Ethos

https://www.operationmilitarykids.org/navy-seal-creed-ethos/

Footnotes:
    (1) Peter Dunstan Blueprint for Revival 2015
        amazon.com.au
    (2) Kingdom Warriors Creed by Peter Dunstan

Chapter 11:

2020 Decade: Multiple Birthings

A Glorious Destiny

I am convinced that any suffering we endure is less than nothing compared to the magnitude of glory that is about to be unveiled within us. The entire universe is standing on tiptoe yearning to see the unveiling of God's glorious sons and daughters! For against its will the universe itself has had to endure the empty futility resulting from the consequences of human sin.But now with eager expectation, all creation longs for freedom from its slavery to decay and to experience with us the wonderful freedom coming to God's children. To this day we are aware of the universal agony and groaning of creation, as if it were the contractions of labour for childbirth.
And it's not just creation. We who have already experienced the first-fruits of the Spirit also inwardly groan as we passionately long to experience our full status as God's sons and daughters –including our physical bodies being transformed. For this is the hope of our salvation.
(Romans 8:18-24 TPT)

*A*s I waited on the Lord, I had an encounter where He showed me that throughout this decade and this new era, there would be an outpouring of Kingdom purposes as each year ushers in *'new births'*. It was like the cascading of breaking waters. Each wave that was released into each new-year, delivered more of heaven into the earth. Aspects and dimensions of heaven will be *birthed* into our world here on earth, in this new decade and throughout this new era.

Just as in a natural birth first you conceive, and then carry the baby for a nine month term as it grows and forms. Finally the membranes in the amniotic sac rupture (or, as we call it 'your water breaks'). Then you give birth and you have new life. I can almost hear all the Mammas say 'Amen!' In the natural birth, when the waters break this signals that the baby is coming.

I believe the Lord has impregnated *Spiritual wombs* of the *"surrendered ready ones"*. That's you, that's me, that includes many intercessors, gatekeepers, the watchmen, the warriors, the five-fold ministers, and the ekklesia. Those of us who are ready to pay the price. We are all called to *birth* and bring forth God's Kingdom purposes.

In the Spirit, I saw the breaking of spiritual waters that cascaded into the earth. I was seeing the *birthing of God's blueprints, plans and purposes into this new era.* It was a *birthing of the things on God's heart.* Birthed through the *'ready ones'* with tried and tested hearts. Those ones who are surrendered and yielded to Him.

As I write this book, I have already heard many reports of people receiving downloads and strategic blueprints for their next assignment, the next step, and the next level of the new dimensions in Christ.

I believe there will be dreams, visions, prayers, declarations and decrees to be actioned and released. There will be new songs, new attitudes, unshakeable faith, hope, and the love of God that will ooze out of you like a weighty substance. It will spill out onto those around you in a great measure of power. This will cause the people around you to fall on their knees and repent, committing their lives to Jesus. I believe this is part of the great end time billion soul harvest that God spoke to the late Bob Jones about when he died and went to heaven (1).

I believe the Lord has been searching to and fro across the earth for the *ready ones*, the *willing ones*, the *sold out, set apart, living sacrifices*. These are the *tried and tested ones*. Are you ready to say 'yes' to the greatest call of God today?

The army of the Lord is waiting for you to join forces with them, for what is coming. Could I encourage you to ask yourself that question, 'am I ready and willing to be a part of one of the greatest awakenings of all time?' This will be a wonderful and powerful move of God? Ask 'how badly do I want this?' 'What am I willing to lay down, to sacrifice?' For there is a price to pay. Let me assure you that the price is nothing compared to the magnitude of glory that is about to be unveiled within you and through you.

> *18 I am convinced that any suffering we endure is less than nothing compared to the magnitude of glory that is about to be unveiled within us.* (Romans 8:18 TPT)

I felt God say to me:

'The Lord is releasing new and fresh vision, with supernatural sharpness and clarity to shift and lift your vision, casting it beyond your wildest imaginations'

There is such a sense of expectancy, increase and of the "exceedingly abundantly more" (see Ephesians 3:20), of what is carried in the wombs of the ready ones.

Get ready, don't miss this significant time and season we are in. He is about to give you a new and fresh vision. He is releasing a supernatural sharpness and clarity of vision to the ready ones. Ready for what, you might ask. Ready for 1 Corinthians 2:9:

> *"What no eye has seen, what no ear has heard, and what no human mind has conceived, the things God has prepared for those who love Him"*
> (1 Corinthians 2:9 NIV).

There are new levels of the miraculous becoming available to you, 'the ready ones.' This is coming to those who want to be a part of this great end time harvest that is about to take place. It is a harvest that no eye has seen before, no ear has heard before, a harvest and move of God that no human mind could even imagine!

It is so important to be found ready in these times, ready to move into position and ready to be sent out, in order to be a part of this move of God which is about to take place and be birthed in the earth!

In December 2019, before the beginning of 2020, the Lord downloaded a prophetic word to me for the 2020 Decade, and the new era. I would like to share it with you and share some of the revelations the Lord has given to me since the publication.

This is what the Lord said and revealed to me:

"As each new-year breaks throughout this decade, it will be like the *'breaking of pregnant waters'* signifying the beginning of a *'new wave of new births.'*

New Year, new era, new wave, new births!

I heard in the Spirit, many people sounding the alarm and announcing:

'My water broke, my water broke'

This was referring to the amniotic sac rupturing to begin the birthing process. There was such excitement and anticipation. The angelic realm and those on earth, all stood in awe of the *magnitude of this miraculous breaking forth*. The scale of this is on a level that "we have not seen", "we have not heard of, nor have we conceived in our hearts and minds".

The sense of Kingdom glory on these *'cascading birthing waters'* is weighty. It carries the Fathers heart and glory in its DNA. The Lord will birth His gloriously rich Kingdom blueprints and plans through you. They are ready and waiting in the Spirit realm to be birthed upon the earth.

The Lord's words to me were:

'I have made pregnant those who seek me diligently. They are pregnant and carry what I am about to birth into the earth'

The Lord had given me this word in December of 2019 to be released in January, at the beginning of the New Year 2020, for the New Decade and this New Era.

I released this word in January and it was published on the Australian Prophetic Council's Facebook Page on 14th January 2020. I believe this message is a now word to set us up for the decade and for the new era.

Now over the next few months into the 2020 year, we heard from seasoned and highly credible prophets who were saying 'we are in a birthing season', 'it's a new era', 'a pregnant pause'.

Tim Sheets, a highly respected Apostolic voice heard from the Lord and in May 2020 he declared we have been in a 'pregnant pause'. He said 'we are moving from a pregnant pause to birthing'. He says 'we are entering into a mega birth season'. Tim also said 'the waters of Pentecost are about to break,' and referred to 'a mega birthing at Pentecost.' (2)

I found this very encouraging and confirmation of the prophetic word I had released at the beginning of the year. So, could I encourage you to consecrate yourself, guard your intimate time with God, and spiritually position yourself to be impregnated with what the Lord is wanting to birth *through you* into this new era. The incubator is found in the secret place with the Lord. Spiritual intimacy with the Lord produces spiritual pregnancy and the Lord births His plans through you. We are not spectators, we are Kingdom Warriors! Amen.

The Lord continued to speak to me:

'This decade will see the release of the miraculous in quantities, in magnitude, and in ways that will surprise and shock the world at large.

The new 2020 decade is marked with greater revelation of His love and grace; multiple manifestations of the miraculous; jaw dropping divine encounters; increased supernatural seeing encounters and interaction with the angelic realm. We are talking about the greater spiritual dimensions.

I believe the Lord revealed to me that the 2020's will be a *decade of the miraculous, a glory decade*, and a decade of *eagle prophets* being birthed and rising through the glory realms to *see* what the Father sees, and to *speak* only what they hear the Father speak. We know that as the darkness of these days attempt to cover the earth, His glory is magnified as we shine brighter than ever before.

I felt the Lord encouraging us to 'take heed of the word of the Lord released through His heart-refined prophetic voices. These are the ones whose hearts are like gold, refined through yielding, sacrifice, and fiery testing. These are the ones found to be pure in heart. Those who are ready to birth, birth, birth, and release the cascading river of life that ushers in the *new* glory realms, bringing revelation of the "knowledge of the glory of God that covers the earth as the waters cover the seas".

Tim Sheets puts it like this 'this is all going to be done in a spiritual atmosphere of greater glory than has ever been seen on the earth' (3)

Here is more of what the Lord revealed to me at the beginning of the decade – 'My glory is being released in power in this new decade and in this new era.'

Expect the breaking of the miraculous, never before encountered. It will cause many to be stopped in their tracks. It will cause a flood of souls to be harvested and transformed for the Kingdom of God! They are harvested and transformed so fast that, they themselves will be harvesting and seeing the Spirit of God at work, *in* them and *through* them, while transforming others *around* them.

So, we can be confident that the 2020 decade and new era will be marked by the glory manifesting in miraculous ways as kingdom blueprints, plans and purposes are birthed into the earth, even as darkness tries to cover the earth. I believe this will see the increase of the knowledge of the glory of God across the earth as the waters cover the sea.

Prayer

Let's just take a moment to pray right now to see a release of greater anticipation and hope and expectation in our hearts. Feel free to just lift your hands, ready to receive as you read and agree in your heart.

Heavenly Father, we as your ambassadors of heaven, come boldly into your throne of grace. Right now we open our hearts afresh to you Lord. We open our heart and Spirit to you alone O Lord. You who can supernaturally do the things we cannot do in the natural. We open up to the impossible becoming possible.

Lord position us, as we purposefully position ourselves before you right now. Lord take us deep into covenant, relational oneness with you, deeper than we have ever been before.

May our hearts merge together now and beat as one with you. May our human Spirit merge completely with you Father, Son and Holy Spirit. May we be so fused into you Lord that we begin to live in new dimensions of who you are, and in new realms of intimacy and glory, through being joined in one spirit with you. Let us be so close to you that our ear is upon your chest God, to hear what you are saying, to know the depths of your heart for our families, our nation, and the nations.

I ask you now Lord God to begin to release an impartation to each one engaged in this prayer. Lord, impart a fresh revelation of the greater dimensions of your everlasting unending love for all people, every tongue, tribe, nation and every generation.

Impart the unshakeable faith of God to believe for '*the breaking forth of the miraculous in ways we have never seen before.*' Impart greater revelation, take us into greater dimensions of who you are and who we are, as ONE with each other, and ONE with you. Prepare us to encounter you today in new and deeper ways. Take us into the more intimate realm with you Lord. In your precious name, we pray. Amen!

Footnotes:

1: Bob Jones: Heavenly Visions and One Billion Youth, 4th October 2013 Web TV Show #4
https://www.youtube.com/watch?v=EtWKDOa2Y7w

2: Tim Sheets | Senior Pastor, Apostle, Author
The Oasis Church, Middletown Ohio
Prophetic Word: It's Birthing Season! | Tim Sheets - YouTube
4th May 2020
https://www.youtube.com/watch?v=OsQ6PWARuHE

3. Prophetic Word: It's Birthing Season! | Tim Sheets - YouTube 4th May 2020

Chapter 12:

New Decade New Era

A New Thing

"Stop dwelling on the past. Don't even remember
these former things. I am doing something new,
something unheard of. Even now it sprouts and grows
and matures. Don't you perceive it?"

(Isaiah 43: 18, 19)

*A*t the end of each year my husband and I love to set aside quality time to spend with the Lord to intentionally seek to hear what He has on His heart and mind for the New Year ahead. This time, we got more than we expected. I received a word for the decade and for the new era we were entering into.

During December 2019, we were driving down a dirt road leading into a nearby National Park. We often go there to pray and hear what God is saying. I was excited as we approached the entrance. I was sensing Father's presence so strongly this day and had such an expectancy in my Spirit to encounter Him in a profound way.

As we were approaching the entrance, I distinctly heard the Lord say these words:

'Go low, go deep, rise and release'

I instantly recognised and felt there was a weightiness on those few words. I said to God, what is that all about?

This is the revelation He gave me:

I believe God is calling the body of Christ to a new dimension of surrender and humility as we *'go low'*. He wants us to be immersed *'deep'* into the secret place of intimacy and into the heart of God, in covenant relationship and oneness with Him. This is where we will be equipped for what is to come. We will then, as the bride *'rise'*, with high ranking authority, to then *'release'* God's kingdom blueprints, plans and purposes on the earth. In doing so, the plans of the enemy will be annihilated.

As these words came to me, I recognised it was a strategic directive for the New Decade and the New Era we have now entered into. We are in a strategic and key time, and significant time in history right now. I believe this is a God strategy that will play a significant role in ushering in the end time Spiritual birthing of heavenly blueprints. So as we embrace, partner with, and activate this strategy in our own lives, and together corporately, I believe we will see a new era of the glory of God and the manifestation of heaven on earth.

Divine Strategy:

"Go Low, Go Deep, Rise and Release

↓

"Spiritual Birthing of Heavenly Blueprints"

↓

New Manifestations of Heaven on Earth

The Strategy

The Lord gave me a strategy in four parts! The strategy is this:

1. Go low
2. Go deep
3. Rise and
4. Release.

This is the Kingdom strategy to see the multiple birthings in this glory decade that will bring forth the eternal life-giving plans of heaven, released in the earth.

As I meditated on this and sought the Lord regarding what it was all about, He expanded on what the strategy looks like and how you and I can partner with His strategy for this new era. By partnering with this, we will be a part of ushering in the multiple new birthings, ushering in the miraculous and increasing the knowledge of the glory of God.

I want to share with you what the Lord revealed to me about *each* of this *four part* strategy.

Strategy #1: 'Go Low'

The Lord dropped this scripture into my Spirit:

> *For I know your power and presence shines on all your lovers. Your glory always hovers over all who bow low before you.* (Psalm 85:9 TPT).

What a promise! As you *'GO LOW'* surrendering all before the Lord, the power and presence of God will shine on you, and the Glory of God will hover all over you as you "bow low before Him". Bowing low before the Lord attracts the glory of God!

Two words came to my mind for the instruction to *'GO LOW'*:

'Humility' and 'surrender'

Not just as we have known it to be, but as we have never known it. The Lord is doing a new thing (see Isaiah 43:19 NIV)

We see keys in the scripture in Proverbs:

> *The source of revelation-knowledge is found as you fall down in* **surrender** *before the Lord. Don't expect to see Shekinah glory until the Lord sees your sincere* **humility**. (Proverbs 15:33 TPT). Emphasis is mine.

We can begin to prepare ourselves for this move of God in these times, by doing what the word says to do – *'fall down in surrender'*. We can ask the Lord questions like 'what can I surrender Lord?' 'What else? How can I love you more?' 'What else needs to be stripped away from me Lord?' Transform us in the surrender.

We can *let* him transform us. Let Him change what needs to change in us. Let Him make us the new wineskin, ready to contain and pour out the new wine in this new era.

What needs to change in me to walk in the *new dimensions of maturity, in true unity, as one family, with one heart, representing the father's heart, in greater oneness with you Lord*?

The Lord spoke to me and said these words:

'Your humble, tender surrender to me reveals the access code to my shekinah glory realm.'

Your humility and unwavering surrender will be the KEY to unlock the door to my unshakeable Kingdom.

This key gives you right of passage to my revelation-knowledge.'

These keys are *ancient keys* to *ancient doors* of wisdom and revelation to be imparted into the present time for this era.

Wow! What a promise, I am taking hold of that, and you can too! There is an access code that the Lord wants to give you. This code will take you into new glory realms, where greater manifestations of the miraculous happen. It is the Shekinah glory.

Shekinah is a Hebrew word. It means: 'dwelling' or 'settling.' I believe God is talking about giving you access into the deeper dwelling place with Him.

I believe there is an invitation to enter into a state of *'settling'* in the divine presence of God like you have not experienced before. Greater access to God's divine presence, and God's manifest presence and glory.

Glory to Glory, to be ever increasing in glory, is to continually be changed and transformed into what you were created to be, to be more and more like Jesus.

So if you want to *encounter Him* in the Shekinah glory realm. If you want the *glory* of God to hover over you, and the *power* and *presence* of God to remain in you, and shine *on* you, *out of* you, *in* you and *through* you, so that all who come into contact with you will encounter Jesus – you can have access to this. Your humility and your surrender are keys to access this.

The Invitation

To receive the access code, there is an invitation for you who are reading this right now. It is an invitation to offer up to the Lord every part of your heart, every part of your life. This means surrendering things like our own thoughts and opinions, any pre-conceived ideas, prejudices, and our natural human ways. It is an invitation to make room for His supernatural ways to supersede our natural inclinations.

Humility and surrender is the key. I believe this is a key that will unlock you to step into the greatest awakening of these times and the promises God has for this nation. This is part of the strategy.

One of the ancient keys to unlock the ancient door and enter into the unshakeable Kingdom of God is to stay the course, and be positioned in a place of surrender. Let nothing shake you from this place. Don't let fear shake you. Don't let the influx of bad news infiltrate your resolve to surrender to Him alone. Don't let the coronavirus shake you from your unwavering place of surrender to the glorious one. But rather, lean into Him and ask Him this question 'how can I partner with what you are doing Lord?'

Jesus, thank you for access to your revelation knowledge. Open the eyes of our understanding afresh right in this moment. We surrender more, right now as you breathe on this time of seeking you. Thank you Jesus! Amen!

What does *'go low'* look like?

For me, it partly looks like having an unbridled commitment to a deepening and intimate relationship with Father, Jesus and Holy Spirit. It looks like spending time cultivating my relationship with the triune God, listening, hearing, laughing, and loving the Godhead; being a friend of Jesus, sitting with, and hanging out with Jesus. It looks like being positioned on my knees, on my face, bowed low, praying, interceding, travailing; turning my heart towards Jesus; meditating on His goodness; reading and studying; talking about, sharing and discussing the word of God. It looks like applying the word of God in my everyday living; consecrating myself; time abiding in His presence; communing with Him, taking communion often; and enjoying deep intimacy with Him.

It looks like dancing with Jesus, going on journeys with Jesus, singing and worshipping Jesus in English and in tongues (see Acts 2:4: Acts 19:6; Mark 16:17;   1 Corinthians 2:10; 1 Corinthians 14:5; 1 Corinthians 14:39). Could I encourage you to ask Jesus, 'what does it look like for me to go low in surrender, yielding to you Lord Jesus?'

Strategy # 2: 'Go Deep'

The second part of the strategy was to *'go deep'*:

Right here, The Lord took me into a VISION:

In the vision, I saw the *lion of the tribe of Judah* running towards me. He picked me up in His mouth and threw me up onto his back. I was now riding with Him. He took me into this white, gold, glory light where we *'appeared to disappear.'*

The sense I had as we *'almost disappeared'* was that this is a new place of covenant relationship and oneness. It is a deep place that Father summons one to by name. It's a glorious place to dwell and abide. There have been many times that I have not wanted to leave this nourishing place.

That's the *'go deep'* – a new place of covenant relationship and oneness with Jesus. It is a place that is deeper in the heart of the Father than we have ever been, and deeper than we have ever known.

The Lord spoke again to me:

As you *Go Deep*, you abide in union with me, in intimate relationship and covenant oneness with me; it is here in this secret place of intimacy, covenant relationship and oneness, when you set time aside to be with me, that I will impregnate you with MY Kingdom vision for the 2020 decade. I will reveal MY plans, MY Kingdom blueprints to you to be released into the earth, through you.

There is a place of intimacy that has never been entered into – This is the deeper place in God – where he speaks to us and reveals His intentions. We must be intentional to seek Him in this place. Yes it will require something to change in us, for Him to transform us, for us to be willing to let him reveal our own character flaws, any bitterness or hatred towards another, and a desire to be refined by Him. He is preparing us to be the bride *without spot, wrinkle, or blemish.*

> [26] *to make her holy and clean, washed by the cleansing of God's word. He did this to present her to himself as a glorious church without a spot or wrinkle or any other blemish. Instead, she will be holy and without fault.* (Ephesians 5:26-27 NLT)

He is not talking about the wrinkles in our human skin – he is talking about the condition of the new wineskin, to contain the new wine for this new era. But there are some parts of our character that are not yet holy or blameless, not yet without fault or flaws or free from impurities. These things we can surrender to Him and let him work on in us, to heal and deliver us. We have some healing to be done, maybe some have hidden bitterness towards another.

The Lord wants to uproot whatever is in us, that he did not ever intend to be in us. Things that do not completely line up with the fathers heart of love. *He created us in His image and likeness* (Genesis 1:27). To be a mature bride for His pleasure, until we become a source of praise to Him – glorious, radiant, beautiful and holy (see Ephesians 5:27 TPT), pure, set apart, and altogether radiant with holiness. What a beautiful, glorious image that is.

Not one of us can say that we are perfect. We all fall short of the glory of God, but Jesus in His mercy, grace, and tender-hearted loving kindness, nurtures us and invites us into the secret place with Him where we can be refined and reformed and transformed to be more like Him. How wonderful is He!

It is in the secret place of intimacy with the Lord that we will be fashioned to be more like him, without spot, wrinkle or blemish. This is all part of the preparation of the Bride of Christ, that's you, that's me, that's all of us. Can you sense the beauty and the urgency on this message in this time?

Two scriptures were highlighted to me relating to this part of the strategy to *'go deep'*:

"I have given them the glory that you gave me, that they may be one as we are one - I in them and you in me … ".(John 17:21-22 NIV)

That is the oneness I speak of.

"I will give you hidden treasures, riches stored in secret places, so that you may know that I am the Lord, the God of Israel, who summons you by name". (Isaiah 45:3 NIV)

He summons you by name today! What a promise, he will give you hidden treasures stored in the secret place! These are the blueprints, plans, and the purposes the Lord wants to release into your neighbourhood, community, city, region, and our nation and even the nations. He wants to do this through you. Will you draw near to Him so He can draw near to you? (See James 4:7, 8 NKJV)

As the year progressed, I heard many seasoned prophets from around the world heralding that we have entered into a time of 'pause'. Some prophesied similar words that we are in a 'Selah' time; or a time to stop and listen and go deeper with God, into the secret place to hear from God like never before.

Strategy #3: 'Rise'

In a vision, I could see a *golden coloured eagle rise*! As I took a closer look, this one eagle was made up of a convergence of many eagles. I sensed it represented eagle prophets rising. It also represented ministers of the word of God, watchmen, intercessors, and five-fold ministers. These are the ones who have gone low in humble surrender, gone deep into the Lords presence, and are ready to *now rise*!

The Lord said to me:

'As you rise on the thermal winds of Holy Spirit, filled with the fullness of MY Spirit- within your womb, you carry a kingdom cargo. Glory, anointing, power, might, counsel, giftings, graces, mantles and my word have been revealed to you and received from the intimate, secret place of oneness with me.'

Can you see how we will be equipped with these things in the *going low* and *going deep*? As we surrender and lean into God, we are being equipped to rise up in great authority.

I believe He said to me:

'As you rise, you take flight and take realms. You will see with eagle eye vision into the gateways to cities, regions and nations. You bring vision to those ones with ears to hear, that you could never imagine possible. The higher you go, the more ground you take. You rise empowered, filled with Kingdom revelation. Within your pregnant womb there is harvest seed of the miraculous. MY Kingdom plans and Kingdom blueprints, sealed with gold, and sealed by your sacrificial surrender. Now ready to be released!'

That brings me to the fourth part of the strategy that the Lord gave me to share.

Strategy #4: 'Release'

The command to '*release*' resounds across the airwaves! As the '*eagle carriers*' rise in convergence, that is you and your sister, your brother in the body of Christ. Every tongue and tribe, a uniting of mantles across denominations, cultures and generations, as we all converge I see the waters break. The golden seal opens, releasing waves and waves of the Lord's glorious goodness. This marks another '*New Wave of New Birthings.*' As this happens each year, there will be more and more of the Kingdom of heaven released into the earth.

As you get the revelation, get equipped and release to others what God gives you, I feel the Lord saying:

'My glory is increased throughout this decade. Each year is marked with cascading New waves of New Birthings of the Kingdom into the earth, saturating my people with awe-striking miracles, as the power of my hand is released upon the earth.'

Miracles are going to come through you. Through your hands, your prayers, your intercession, and your fasting, and by you partnering with those you are aligned to. As you are obedient to release what the Lord has given to you, it will glorify Him and we will see His glory increased throughout the nations in this new decade and era.

I believe He says:

Large land masses will be struck with My goodness. My fast flowing love will be like a flood. No longer will I be denied, souls will come flooding in.

I believe these are the times we are in. The goodness of God, the love of God will become awakened to us in new and unimaginable ways. This is a glimpse of the miraculous power of God that will be released into the earth in this new era. His love and tender hearted goodness, flowing through you, will cause many souls to surrender their lives, and lay down their lives to take up the cross and follow Jesus.

The Lord spoke again:

'Release the precious Kingdom cargo, release the word of the Lord. Release my wisdom, and release my direction. Put my kingdom blueprints and plans into manifest action. Declare, decree, announce, and proclaim the gospel in all cities, regions, nations and all spheres of influence. Release my glory as you take dominion and govern the earth.'

We will begin to see whole blueprints that the Lord will supernaturally reveal to us, begin to be put into action. They will be filled with His divine wisdom and strategies, and draw many to Jesus.

This scripture was quickened to my Spirit:

I empower princes to rise and take dominion and generous ones to govern the earth. (Proverbs 8:16 TPT)

In Jesus mighty name Amen.

So Kingdom warriors and ambassadors of heaven, the Lord is looking for those who are ready. He wants to equip you for the greatest days ahead of us. Let me encourage us to go low, go deep, humbly surrender to Him. Listen for the revelation he wants to reveal to you, gather with other believers, dive deep into the word of God and worship Him with everything in you. Spend time in His presence, abide in Him and seek His face.

This is a time to walk more closely than ever with the family of God and with the Lord himself.

Practical Steps

Could I encourage you to live this strategy to *"Go low, Go deep, Rise and Release"*, not just for today, but throughout the 2020 decade and throughout this new era.

Let us humble ourselves, guard our integrity by asking Holy Spirit to reveal to us what we need to surrender. The aim is to yield and surrender all. May we take time to be with Him in the secret place of intimacy, covenant relationship and oneness with the Lord. May we be those sacrificing all else to cultivate our love *for* Him and our relationship *with* Him. Steward well what the Lord reveals to you.

Set yourselves within a family of wise counsel, a company of friends and lovers of Jesus. At the right time, being accountable to those you are aligned with, rise up and release the word of the Lord through teaching, preaching, intercession, declaration, decrees, proclamation, impartation and activation. Take your place, alongside every tongue and tribe, nation and generation, to take dominion and govern the earth.

Expect a great outpouring of God's glory, power, wisdom, counsel and might in this decade and throughout the era, in new and shocking ways that have never been seen before.

I want to take a moment right here, if I may, to pray and release that over you. I invite you to engage your heart to receive from the Lord.

Prayer:

Lord we give you all honour and all glory, as we declare our never ending love for you Lord Jesus. We say Lord, release us into new depths of intimacy with you, new levels of greater revelation of who you are and who we are in you. Release us into new levels of maturity and surrender to you. Release us into new levels of humility, new depths with you Lord, plumbing the depths of your word and your heart. Release us into the deeper places in prayer, intercession, new depths of travail ready to birth your kingdom plans and purposes, ready to receive from you Lord.

Lord make us ready to be refined, reformed, changed and transformed by you. Ready to enter into a new level of healing and wholeness, so that we can love your people with your Father's heart. Prepare us to know you in a way that we've never known you. Prepare us for more of you in our life. Ready to release more of you through our life. In Jesus name I receive this impartation of your grace to do this Lord. Thank You Lord Jesus, Amen!

Your takeaway from this chapter at any given time in this new era is to engage this strategy. Spend time with the Lord and meditate on His word. Ask God what does it look like for me to 'go low', 'go deep', so that I can 'rise', ready to then 'release' what you give me to release into my sphere of influence and beyond?

T   surrender all to be **totally** available to respond to the Commander of the Lord of Hosts at any moment in time.

R   **Revere** Him, in awe of His Glory and allow Him to strip you of the baggage that will weigh you down

U   be found in the secret place, **undetected** by the enemy

T   be open and ready to be equipped, **take** on whatever weapons the Lord puts in your quiver. Be ready to charge, on His command, to action the blueprints, plans and purposes he reveals to you

H   stay **humble** before Him, going deep into His presence and heart. Expect Him to equip you for the task, for the assignment, for the battle, for the victory. Be ready to rise up and release what He gives you to release.

Practical Strategies

Fix your eyes on Jesus. Fiercely focus on 'go low, go deep' going forward. Join together in prayer. You can pray every day, either on your own, or with a friend. Take communion often, even every day if led to. Consecrate yourselves to God, and make yourself available to God in this time. Ask him to transform you in these times of prayer and listening to him, worshipping him. Get grounded and securely anchored in the word of God. Get yourself equipped to move out as the Lord leads you. Go into your neighbourhoods, community, city and nation to share the word of God.

Key Scriptures

- 1 Corinthians 2:9 (NIV)
"What no eye has seen, what no ear has heard, and what no human mind has conceived"— the things God has prepared for those who love him. We cannot begin to imagine the magnitude of the move of God that is beginning. We just need to get ourselves ready and be willing. He will use the ready ones.

- (Psalm 85:9 TPT)
For I know your power and presence shines on all your lovers. Your glory always hovers over all who **bow low** before you.

- (Proverbs 15:33)
The **source** of **revelation-knowledge** is found as you **fall down** in **surrender** before the Lord. Don't expect to see Shekinah glory until the Lord sees your sincere **humility**. HUMILITY IS THE KEY, A NEW DEPTH OF HUMILITY

- (John 17:21-22)
I have given them the glory that you gave me, that they may be one as we are one
"I in them and you in me". – THIS IS COVENANT ONENESS WITH GOD – WITH
FATHER, SON AND HOLY SPIRIT

- (Isaiah 45:3)
I will give you hidden treasures, riches stored in secret places, so that you may know that I am the Lord, the God of Israel, who summons you by name.

- (Proverbs 8:16 TPT)
I empower princes to rise and take dominion and generous ones to govern the earth.

Decree with me:

I invite you to decree with me. Speak these decrees out loud, agree in your heart and receive them by faith:

- Lord God I decree that you have prepared for me, what no eye has seen, what no ear has heard, and what no human mind has conceived" custom made for me. (see1 Corinthians 2:9 NIV)

- I declare and I decree that your power and your presence shines on me Lord God Almighty, your glory hovers over me right now as I humbly bow before you (see Psalm 85:9 TPT)

- I declare and decree tonight Lord that I choose to fall down in surrender to you afresh Almighty God. I declare that you are the source of all revelation knowledge to me - right here, right now, in a new, deeper and greater way. Take me into new dimensions of your perfect love. (see Proverbs 15:33)

- I declare and decree that I encounter your Shekinah glory and see your glory manifest in and around my life, in my family, in my community, city, town, region, nation and out to the nations. Lord see my humility and release this to be so (see Proverbs 15:33)

- I decree that we have the glory that you Father gave to Jesus. I decree that we are one with Father, Son and Holy Spirit and we are one with each other. I decree that I am in covenant oneness with Father (see John 17:21-22)

- I decree that right now Lord you are releasing to me hidden treasures, and riches stored in secret places. I decree that

I have full access to these, to receive and release. I decree that you are Lord, the God of Israel and you summon me by my name. In Jesus precious name. (see Isaiah 45:3)

- I decree that I have risen with Christ and I am taking dominion to govern the earth. (Proverbs 8:16 TPT)

- I declare and decree that I consecrate myself to you and I will see your blueprints birthed and put into action. I will see your plans executed. I will see your purposes fulfilled. I will see your glory fill the earth as the waters cover the sea.

In your Mighty name Jesus!! Amen.

Conclusion

*M*y assignment in writing this book was to:

- Communicate the significant role First Nations people have in the awakening of our nation for revival, reformation and transformation in this nation and nations.
- highlight ancient keys created from time long ago that will unlock this new era
- release strategies to you to access and apply these ancient keys
- And to unlock a new sound that is rising from the land in this new era.

They are ancient keys to the new era. These ancient keys unlock a door to the end time harvest. They are ancient keys to the new sound rising from the land.

The new sound rising from the land is a sound of the *diverse united bride* readying herself. It is the sound of the *remnant army rising* to overthrow foreign kingdoms. It is the sound of *unity, family and oneness* like never before.

This book is an invitation:

- It is an invitation to *'go low'* in humility, surrendered as we humble ourselves, pray, and seek His face like never before and watch Him heal our land.
- It is and invitation to *'go deep'* into new dimensions of intimacy, consecrating ourselves, being refined and reformed, a place where the secrets of Fathers heart is revealed to us. A place of being equipped.

- It is and invitation to then *'rise'* with high ranking authority and lightning bolt power.
- It is an invitation to *'go low, go deep, rise and release'* the Kingdom blueprints, plans and purposes conceived in the supernatural to be birthed in the natural as heaven and earth align.

This book is a call:

- It is a call to First Nation people to *arise and lead* for God's glory
- It is a call for the voice of the First Nation Five-Fold to *arise and resound* throughout the land.
- It is a call for the *Tribal Warrior Bride* to ready herself.
- It is a call to *unity* in the Body of Christ.
- It is a call to *convergence* of every tongue, tribe, language and nation
- It is a call to *unite and ignite* to set this nation ablaze for Jesus
- It is a call for the *burning ones* to be sent out to *set nations ablaze* with end time revival fire, bringing reformation and transformation to nations.

Will you accept the invitation?
Will you answer the call with your '*YES*'?

Let us be the burning ones to set the nations ablaze.

Australia, you are my burning one, it has now begun!

Meet Katie Dunstan:

Katie Dunstan cultivates an unbridled commitment to a deepening intimacy with Jesus. Out of this, the Lord has established her as a prophetic voice to the nation.

Katie is a First Nations Gomeroi Murri Yinnar (Aboriginal woman of Gomeroi tribe) from Walhallow, also known as Caroona Mission, in North Western NSW Australia. Her people are the Gomeroi people. As a First Nations Christian leader, she is passionate to empower and see God's voice amplified and Jesus glorified, through the First Nations voices of the land across the globe. She believes this is a key to awaken nations and to ignite revival, reformation and transformation.

She is a First Nations preacher and prophetic revivalist who loves to witness the Spirit of God unite and ignite nations to be set ablaze for Jesus. She travels throughout Australia and South Eastern Asia equipping others as she ministers in communities, conferences, open air crusades, and Churches. Alongside her husband, she serves her community and nations as founder of Breakfree Australia; a Pioneer of 'Prophetic Voices of the Land' in Australia; she is an Author and Speaker. Katie is married to Peter, and together they enjoy cultivating and hosting God's presence and housing His glory in Bendemeer, NSW Australia.

Katie Dunstan   Author: Speaker: Prophetic Revivalist

Facebook: Breakfree Australia
E: breakfreeaust@gmail.com

AVAILABLE FOR PREACHING AND TRAINING

To invite Katie as a Guest Speaker:
Email: breakfreeaust@gmail.com

Co-Author: Healing Wounded Hearts: Holy Spirit Directed Inner Healing - Available @_amazon.com.au or amazon.com

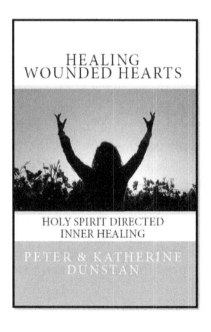

Made in the USA
Las Vegas, NV
06 May 2023

71679857R00154